FINDING GOD'S
Presence in Our Life

FINDING GOD'S
Presence in Our Life

Faith, Prayer, and Action

PETER M. KALELLIS

Paulist Press
New York / Mahwah, NJ

Unless otherwise noted, the Scripture quotations contained herein are from the New Revised Standard Version: Catholic Edition, Copyright © 1989 and 1993, by the Division of Christian Education of the National Council of the Churches of Christ in the United States of America. Used by permission. All rights reserved.

Cover image: REMBRANDT Harmenszoon van Rijn, *The Return of the Prodigal Son* (detail), c. 1669. Oil on canvas. The Hermitage, St. Petersburg. Taken from Web Gallery of Art/Wikimedia Commons. Used with permission.

Cover design by Tamian Wood
Book design by Lynn Else

Library of Congress Cataloging-in-Publication Data

Kalellis, Peter M.
    Finding God's presence in our life : faith, prayer, and action / Peter M. Kalellis.
        pages cm
    ISBN 978-0-8091-4976-6 (pbk. : alk. paper) — ISBN 978-1-58768-589-7 (ebook)
    1. Christian life. 2. Presence of God. I. Title.
    BV4501.3.K354 2016
    248.4—dc23

                                                                    2015028215

ISBN 978-0-8091-4976-6 (paperback)
ISBN 978-1-58768-589-7 (e-book)

Published by Paulist Press
997 Macarthur Boulevard
Mahwah, New Jersey 07430

www.paulistpress.com

Printed and bound in the
United States of America

To my loving wife, Pat (Panagiota),
my best friend and supportive soulmate,
and our daughter Katina,
a dedicated caregiver

Contents

CONTENTS

Prologue

There are two main approaches to improving the quality of our life. The first is to be mindful of our external conditions and expectations, cultural and societal influences, and see how we can make them match our goals. The second is to take a profound look into ourselves and realize that *we are not simply physical beings who "eat, drink, and be merry, for tomorrow we die."* We are spiritual beings with a soul and purpose in life, destined for a life beyond this one.

Today, there is a deep longing within our human nature for something more, something different, and something better. Most people agree that we like to have more beauty in our lives, more time for entertainment and fun, more money, and more of an opportunity to enjoy life in its fullness and vitality.

Partly because of not knowing how to begin finding which way to go and partly out of fear of changes we might have to make, we have a hard time committing to take care of our inner self, our soul. During four decades as a psychotherapist, I have often heard clients remark that they are experiencing emptiness, that they are vaguely depressed and disillusioned about life and relationships, and that they feel a need for personal fulfillment and emotional satisfaction. These concerns are a reflection of the soul's hunger for spirituality. An accomplished attorney admitted that, while outwardly successful, he felt disturbingly empty inside. His professional accomplishments were very flattering to the ego, but his inner self yearned for spiritual nourishment. Many people comment that the rewards that society has to offer—including prestige, power, money, sex, entertainment, and material goods—are ultimately distractions and potential hindrances to living a more meaningful, fulfilling, and rewarding life.

The waiting rooms of psychiatrists, psychologists, and marriage therapists are filled with rich and successful clients who, in their forties or fifties, suddenly wake up to the fact that a plush suburban home, expensive cars, and even an Ivy League education are not enough to bring peace of mind and make them happy. Although they recognize that material success may not bring happiness, they still engage in an endless struggle to reach external goals, expecting that they will improve their lives.

Wealth, status, and power have become in our culture all-too-powerful symbols of happiness. When we see people who are rich, famous, or good-looking, we tend to assume that their lives are rewarding and that if only we could acquire some of those same symbols, we would be much happier.

Suppose we succeed in becoming richer or more powerful. Our life may improve for a while. We may even impress others with who we are or what we own. But the bottom line is not what others think of us but rather how we feel about ourselves and what happens to us. To gain inner peace and contentment, we need to turn inward and cultivate our inner self. To quote Epicurus, a fourth-century BC Greek philosopher, "It is never too early or too late to care for the well-being of the soul."*

An increasing number of people feel a yearning for personal fulfillment and spiritual growth. They are making an effort to add to their daily living a new dimension, a spiritual activity that makes them feel better. By embracing and practicing a faith, they feel emotionally and physically healthier and better motivated.

---

*Epicurus, *Letter to Menoeceus*, 122.

They sense a desire to have close personal relationships with family, friends, and community. They want their lives to contribute to the well-being of others.

This book is not about making you a theologian or a saint. It is about learning to live in God's presence. Each chapter is designed to make you aware of God in your life and offers the feeling of love, joy, and peace that you will experience in God's presence.

Acknowledgments

I would like to thank the following:

My God who continues to inspire me and bless my life with the desire and the energy to write.

My family, children and grandchildren, friends and relatives, for their continued support and belief in my ministry and writing. In particular, I thank my wife, Pat, whose love, support, and care, at home and while away, keeps me grounded.

Finally, Mark-David Janus, CSP; Paul McMahon; and the dedicated team at Paulist Press for continuing to be interested in my words and make them public.

FAITH

Faith is to believe what you do not see; the reward
of this faith is to see what you believe.

       —Saint Augustine

CHAPTER 1

The Presence of God

HOW WE PERCEIVE GOD is a serious issue for every person. Most of us are aware that we cannot define God. Our finite minds cannot possibly conceive the infinite and incomprehensible power that we call *God*. The Gospels claim that God is love. He wants us all to have fruitful, meaningful lives. If we exclude God from our lives, then the possibility of an effective relationship with God is limited.

Jesus' response to the Samaritan woman, "God is spirit, and those who worship him must worship him in spirit and truth" (John 4:24), helps us understand the presence of God. To sense the presence of God, our efforts must be spiritual. Physically, we cannot see or touch God, but the spirit within us can. As we develop our spiritual life, we will begin to feel God's presence. The Apostle Paul shows us how to develop our spiritual life. In Galatians 5:22–23, he describes the fruit of the Holy Spirit, which is God's gift to all people. But this fruit can become dormant, unless we make an effort to cultivate it. The fruit of the Spirit is a behavioral manifestation of a Christian's transformed life. In order to mature as believers, it is necessary to understand the following nine attributes or fruits of the Holy Spirit, gradually trying to apply them in our everyday life.

Love. "God is love" (1 John 4:8, 16). Love can be the source of great joy when there are no strings attached to the loving process, when people show respect for one another's personality, share responsibilities, and are interested in each other's well-being. Spontaneous love comes from within and lasts for a long time. Once it starts, it must be maintained, nurtured, and reinforced; otherwise it fades and dies. And so we have a choice to rely on the love God has for us. "Those who abide in love abide in God, and God abides in them" (1 John 4:16). Through Jesus Christ, our greatest goal is to do all things in love. "Love is patient; love is kind; love is not envious or boastful or arrogant or rude. It does not insist on its own way; it is not irritable or resentful; it does not rejoice in wrongdoing, but rejoices in the truth. It bears all things, believes all things, hopes all things, endures all things. Love never ends" (1 Cor 13:4–8).

Joy. Joy is a disposition of the heart, the center of all emotions. It is a state of the mind that is devoid of fear. The happiness of the world is conditional and temporary. For a while it may safeguard us materially, providing ample material goods that please our physical existence, but it doesn't satisfy our soul. The joy that our Creator promises is beyond our human understanding. It is an inner satisfaction, a contentment that only the soul experiences. However, to attain this God-given joy, we need to explore areas where we don't feel content and come to terms with aspects of life that are beyond our control. "The joy of the LORD is your strength" (Neh 8:10). And the Letter to the Hebrews reminds us, "Let us run with perseverance the race that is set before us, looking to Jesus the pioneer and perfecter of our faith, who for the sake of the joy that was set before him endured the cross, disregarding its shame, and has taken his seat at the right hand of the throne of God" (12:1–2).

Peace. Everyone we meet is a son or a daughter of a loving God, involved with his or her own struggle in search of inner peace. By our conscious choices, we can move from alienation to a community, from despair to creativity, from passivity to participation, from stagnation to learning, and from cynicism to caring. We may think that we are powerless, helpless, and impotent. Yet the reality is that we—as individuals compassionately working in cooperation with one another—stand a good chance to have a healthy life and be able to attain reasonable peace. "Therefore, since we are justified by faith, we have peace with God through our Lord Jesus Christ" (Rom 5:1). "May the God of hope fill you with all joy and peace in believing, so that you may abound in hope by the power of the Holy Spirit" (15:13).

Long-suffering (patience). "Patience is a virtue." We're all familiar with this cliché, and many of us know that patience is listed by Paul in Galatians 5:22–23 among the fruits of the Spirit. So there's no disputing that a Christian person ought to be patient. But as with most of the virtues, the biblical writers assume that we know what patience is and don't give an explicit definition. Perhaps, in defining patience, we could cite a few examples, starting with the basic definition of *patience* as "waiting without complaint." Jesus, for example, was very patient with his disciples. They were sometimes thickheaded and slow to believe. Even from a merely human standpoint, we can see how frustrating it must have been to interact daily with these men. "May you be made strong with all the strength that comes from his glorious power, and may you be prepared to endure everything with patience" (Col 1:11) and "with all humility and gentleness, with patience, bearing with one another in love" (Eph 4:2).

Gentleness (kindness). In his Letter to the Colossians, Paul admonishes us: "Clothe yourselves with compassion, kindness, humility, meekness, and patience. Bear with one another and, if anyone has a complaint against another, forgive each other; just as the Lord has forgiven you, so you also must forgive" (3:12–13). A kind disposition is possible precisely because the Holy Spirit has given us a new heart. This transformation of the

Spirit is emphasized in Titus: "He saved us, not because of any works of righteousness that we had done, but according to his mercy, through the water of rebirth and renewal by the Holy Spirit" (3:5). We just don't get up in the morning and decide to be kind. Even the best intentions fail if we rely on our own strength. St. Paul called kindness a fruit of the Spirit because it cannot be grown effectively without the Spirit's continuing work in our lives. He encourages us to "be filled with the Spirit" (Eph 5:18) and to live in "purity, knowledge, patience, kindness, holiness of spirit, genuine love, truthful speech, and the power of God; with the weapons of righteousness for the right hand and for the left" (2 Cor 6:6–7).

Goodness. The fruit of the Spirit is goodness. The word *goodness* or the phrase *a good job* refers to something that meets a certain standard, or someone's expectations. It fulfills a goal. Furthermore, the meaning of goodness often depends on the context. A good book is different for different people and purposes. A good book for scholarly research is quite different from a good book for bedtime reading, and good recreation for one person may not be for another. Finally, a good heart is sincere, honest, kind, and moral. But who defines morality? For Christians, God is the One who defines moral goodness and sets the standards and the expectations that must be met. The Scriptures reveal an ultimate and absolute definition of *goodness.* "To this end we always pray for you, asking that our God will make you worthy of his call and will fulfill by his power every good resolve and work of faith" (2 Thess 1:11), "for the fruit of the light is found in all that is good and right and true" (Eph 5:9).

Faith (faithfulness). "O LORD, you are my God; / I will exalt you, I will praise your name; / for you have done wonderful things, / plans formed of old, faithful and sure" (Isa 25:1). St. Paul reminds and reassures the community of Ephesus about the power of faith saying, "I pray that, according to the riches of his glory, he may grant that you may be strengthened in your inner being with power through his Spirit, and that Christ may dwell in your hearts through faith, as you are being rooted and grounded in love" (Eph 3:16–17). Both Isaiah and Paul inspire us to contemplate the power of faith. Faith is possibly the single most important element of the Christian life.

Meekness. While the dictionary describes *meekness* as docile, overly compliant, spiritless, yielding, or tame, the Bible says, "Blessed are the meek, for they will inherit the earth" (Matt 5:5). What is Christian meekness? The Spirit of God adorns the humble person with a multiplicity of graces. The work of the Holy Spirit is not only astonishing, but amazing. The Holy Spirit makes the heart meek, pure, understanding, peaceable, and so on. The graces therefore are compared to fine needlework; intricate and various in its textures and colors (see Ps 45:14). In these words, there is the duty of meekness—and that duty, like the dove, brings an olive leaf in its mouth, as in the time of Noah, signaling peace. The proposition implies that meek people are blessed people: "They will inherit the earth." In spiritual terms, there is a *twofold meekness*: meekness toward God and meekness toward people. Meekness is reacting calmly, without swelling or murmuring, under the adverse dispensations of divine providence: "It is the LORD; let him do what seems good to him" (1 Sam 3:18). The meek-spirited Christian says thus, "Everything is yours; do with it what you will."* God sees what is best for me, whether fertile or barren soil. Let God do his work as he wishes; it suffices that God has done it.

Meekness is a grace whereby we are enabled by the Spirit of God to moderate our angry passions. The philosopher calls it a virtue; St. Paul calls it a grace and therefore reckons it among the fruit of the Spirit (see Gal 5:22). Meekness is of a divine origin.

---

*Saint Ignatius Loyola, "Suscipe," http://www.bc.edu/bc_org/prs/stign/prayers.html.

By it we are enabled to moderate our passions. By nature, the heart is like a troubled sea, periodically casting forth the foam of anger and wrath. Meekness calms the passions. It sits as moderator in the soul, quieting and giving check to its distempered motions. As the moon serves to temper and allay the heat of the sun, so Christian meekness allays the heat of passion. Meekness of spirit not only fits us for communion with God but for civil converse with people, and thus among all the graces, it holds first place. Spiritual meekness has a divine beauty and sweetness and consists in three things: bearing injuries, forgiving injuries, and recompensing good for evil. "My friends, if anyone is detected in a transgression, you who have received the Spirit should restore such a one in a spirit of gentleness. Take care that you yourselves are not tempted" (Gal 6:1).

Temperance (self-control). "For this very reason, you must make every effort to support your faith with goodness, and goodness with knowledge, and knowledge with self-control, and self-control with endurance, and endurance with godliness, and godliness with mutual affection, and mutual affection with love" (2 Pet 1:5–7). These are the characteristics of the fruit of the Spirit. As they become a part of our daily life, we feel better about ourselves and others. Consequently, we radiate integrity, trustworthiness, and a depth of character. We don't rely on personality, intimidation, or trumped-up enthusiasm to win us over. We're not talking about perfection, for we still have the flesh with which to contend. We can be as unkind and insensitive as anybody else, but when we realize our offense, we are quick to apologize and seek forgiveness. Through the power of the Holy Spirit, we can rise above our destructive desires. We find that tuning in to God's presence bears spiritual fruit even during difficult times.

When we abide in Christ and allow him to live his life

through us, the result is a character that endures despite the adversities of life. In summary, the fruit of the Spirit includes:

LOVE—for those who do not love in return.

JOY—in the midst of painful circumstances.

PEACE—when something you were counting on doesn't come through.

PATIENCE—when things aren't going fast enough for you.

KINDNESS—toward those who treat you unkindly.

GOODNESS—toward those who have been intentionally insensitive to you.

FAITHFULNESS—when friends have proven unfaithful.

GENTLENESS—toward those who have handled you roughly.

SELF-CONTROL—in the midst of intense temptation.

While unconditional love in a marriage or friendship shines brightest in the midst of differences, in a similar way, the fruit of the Spirit demonstrates its divine source when circumstances and relationships take a turn for the worse. It is then that the source of the Christian's abiding character is found deep within. When all the crutches and props are kicked away and the believer is still standing, no one can argue that his uniqueness was simply a by-product of his environment. Believers who are aware of the fruit of the Spirit don't win every battle. Doubt, temptation, hurt, and disappointment trip them up from time to time. But they don't dwell on their missteps. They refocus their attention on the big picture, acknowledging the truth that their peace is from the Lord. Then they move on, knowing that "to set the mind on the Spirit is life and peace" (Rom 8:6).

FOR CONSIDERATION

1. The fruit of the Spirit can take you by surprise. You may have seen this happen many times, especially in the lives of new believers. When you shift your focus from self to the Holy Spirit, you notice a difference in yourself. The results are of an unexpected nature: true change—and "fruit that will last" (John 15:16).

2. You don't produce the fruit of the Holy Spirit; you *discover* it. It is a grace. For example, you will finish a debate with your kids and realize you didn't raise your voice. You will walk away from a heated conversation and think, *Wow, I didn't lose my temper.* You will be asked to go somewhere you have no business going, and you will hear yourself saying, "No, thank you." Transformation happens only when you surrender to the promptings of the Holy Spirit.

3. Eventually, you will realize that there is something different, though not because you set out to change. Remember, the fruit of the Spirit is not something you work to attain. It's something that is given to you. It is a gift from God. You may recall what Jesus said to his disciples at the Last Supper: "And I will ask the Father, and he will give you another Advocate, to be with you forever" (John 14:16).

4. Sometimes we grow impatient in our lives when we don't see the spiritual growth we would like to see. It is important to remember that spiritual fruit doesn't grow overnight. It takes time. If you were to plant an apple tree on Monday, you could scarcely expect to enjoy a fresh apple by Friday. Like any visible fruit, the virtues of the Holy Spirit that are part of your life don't become visible overnight. This kind of fruit takes time to grow.

5. Spiritual power is the divine energy that the Holy Spirit is willing to express in and through us. It is the divine authority needed to carry out the work our Lord Jesus has called us to do. We cannot "harness" the power of the Holy Spirit. This power is not just for priests, preachers, evangelists, or people who work in special ministry; rather, it is available to every believer who willingly surrenders each moment in submission and obedience to the Holy Spirit.

CHAPTER 2

The True Self

THROUGH THE FRUIT of the Holy Spirit, your own spirit—God's gift within you—is enriched as you cultivate its nine attributes: love, joy, peace, long-suffering, kindness, goodness, faith, meekness, and temperance.

Pursuing a spiritual life is a personal choice. Rather than beginning with dogmas and incomprehensible theories about God and the invisible world, start from where you are and simply work on the faith that you already have, even if it is small. In the process, you will discover that God nurtures your faith. Some people use religion to avoid the reality of their own life. Some may be fearful of meeting their true self, which translates into psychological fear; others resort to abstract rituals or take refuge in spiritual thoughts and feelings to avoid confronting themselves and their problems.

We come to God through careful self-observation and sincere self-knowledge. We don't tear ourselves down—how terrible and sinful we are, referring to a repertoire of mistakes and bad choices that we have made—to evoke sympathy or to admit how aware we are of our worthlessness. Usually, when we sin or violate the law, we know what we are doing, but we don't understand how much God loves us. Hence we are still innocent through ignorance.

We don't find out what God expects from us in the lofty ideals we set for ourselves—bragging that we pray frequently, confess our sins, fast, and attend church regularly, or that we participate in philanthropic and missionary activities. While these wonderful activities may give us comfort and pleasure, our motive is to "look better" in the eyes of others and of God. But do high ideals make us more spiritual? If we make a large donation to a charitable cause, do we feel any closer to God? At best it makes us feel appreciated.

Simple spirituality suggests that we can discover God's will for us—that we can find our vocation, our purpose in life—only if we have the courage to descend into our reality, accept who we truly are, and deal with our passions, drives, needs, and wishes.

The basic and most fundamental challenge of the spiritual life is accepting the hidden and dark self by which we tend to identify all the evil that is in us. We must discern the evil growth of our actions from the good ground of the soul. And we must prepare that ground so that a new life can grow within us, beyond our knowledge and beyond our conscious control.

The sacred attitude is one of reverence, awe, and silence before the mystery that begins to take place within us when we become aware of our inmost self. In silence, hope, expectation, and unknowing, the person of faith abandons himself or herself to the divine will: not to an arbitrary and magic power whose decrees must be spelled out from cryptic ciphers, but to the stream of reality and life itself. The sacred attitude is, then, one of acceptance and deep respect for the reality in us, in whatever new form it may present itself.

As human beings, our Creator has endowed us with tremendous powers of resilience, and we owe it to ourselves and our world to claim them. Otherwise, we have a hard time interacting with others. In an intimate relationship, at some point, we might seriously hurt a loving person or that loving person might hurt us. Maintaining a good relationship depends on both having the resilience to forgive, forget, bounce back, and live in some joy and happiness *despite* having been hurt and wounded. To some degree, all of us have been wounded. From the moment we emerge from the womb, in ways physical and emotional, we get dropped, burned, rejected, and abandoned. Nobody reaches adulthood without deep scars. The damage may be permanent, but it is not fatal.

God wishes salvation—total recovery from suffering—for every one of us. If we believe in the power of love to heal and to create freely its own response, surely God's perfect love will eventually bring even the most hardened disbeliever to accept it. If human love, weak and imperfect as it may be, can melt hard hearts, won't God's perfect love eventually penetrate any resistance?

The way to God leads through our weaknesses and powerlessness. When we are stripped of all power, we discover what God has in mind for us, what God can make of us when he fills us completely with divine grace. When our spirituality is idealistic, we react to human weaknesses. We react to anger or rage, and repress those feelings. We try to be friendly and balanced at all times and control our rage. When our spirituality is humble, we sense our rage and wonder what God is saying through it. Perhaps our rage is pointing to some deep injury. Perhaps in your anger you encounter the wounded child within who reacts with impotent fury to harm done to you by your parents or teachers or some insensitive adults.

In some cases, your anger could be the energy to free yourself from the power of others, so as to be more open to God. Rage is thus not automatically bad; it could be showing you the way to your true self.

Through your anger, you come into contact with yourself, through the descent into your reality. Through your anger, you come into contact with the source of your strength, as God's Spirit bubbles up within you. And so your anger leads you to God, who wishes to give you life. Wherever your greatest problem lies is also the site of your greatest opportunities; that is where your spiritual life begins. There you come into contact with your true essence, which yearns for life and growth. It's only through your true self that you can sense the presence of God.

Many psychologists use the term *self* to describe our common human experience of having a unique center that we identify as being our true "me." Most people call it: "my soul," "my heart," "my innermost being," "my true self," "my center," "who I truly am," "the true me." We experience this self as the vital core of our inner world.

The self is the author of our thoughts, feelings, actions, fantasies, dreams, and hopes. It is the seat of subjectivity, the center of our initiative, and the source of our creative presence in the world. Above all, the self is generative; it renews and enriches our sense of being alive. If we love our self and love other people, we are living out of our real self and we are being spiritual. If we hate our self, reject our self, or idealize our self as perfect, we are living out of our false self, which can cause anxiety and be an obstacle to being spiritual.

The false self has its origins in the family where our life began and developed. If the family did not allow us to express our true thoughts and feelings, we created a false self in order to be accepted and loved by our parents and other family members. Later, we brought this false self to our school and to our peers in order to be accepted and possibly liked. We repressed our true self, the genuine thoughts and feelings, or rather we stored them in our unconscious. Staying safe and looking good then became of paramount importance. To this end, children and even adults become what will please and protect the false self, rather than who they really feel like on the inside.

Family members silently collude in creating this false sense of normalcy. The false self is an adaptive—actually maladaptive—reaction to a dysfunctional situation. It is largely unconscious; the persons with the false self often never know that it's false, and if you were to challenge them, they would see you as the problem, not themselves, and would probably set about analyzing your need to criticize. If you are bold enough to confront, take on, or critique a false self's behavior, the false self is there to hide, ward off, or cope with unacknowledged pain. And when you challenge the behavior, whether it be compulsive talking, joking, chronic cuteness, or intellectual superiority, you challenge the pain. The hidden hurt is triggered or touched, and anger or retaliation may ensue. *The false self is the source of all unhappiness.* The false self, or ego, leads to destructive thinking and acting. Learning to overcome your ego and to live from your true self is critical for spiritual transformation.

Your true self is how you feel when nobody's watching. It is where your deepest thoughts live. It is what you ultimately think of yourself, how you treat yourself, and what you fear others might see inside you. It is your most native and real personality.

FOR CONSIDERATION

1. When we accept reality without fighting it or trying to adjust it in order to match our needs, we have better peace of mind. Total acceptance cannot really be completely explained, because it is a result of harmonizing emotions with logic, a process that takes place within a person's mind.

2. Many people have experienced in the course of their life total acceptance with a sense of resilience and regained peace of mind. Accepting yourself totally has nothing to do with your worth. You are worthy because God, your Creator, has accepted you totally and unconditionally; he is love and he loves you as his daughter or son.

3. Some people reject themselves because they cannot see themselves as God's creation or as good enough. They only see their flaws and weaknesses, not their beauty, potential, and strength. Self-acceptance is the spiritual act of becoming aware that we are God's creation.

4. In our lifetime, corrections and improvements might be needed, but they can only be done in the spirit of gentleness and love. As you try to generate compassion for others, remember that you are one of them. You have to be loving,

strong, confident, and accepting of yourself before accepting others.

5. Hear your own voice—the voice that comes from within your soul and depends on your character and your nature. It will either encourage you to take even more positive actions in your life or discourage your current situation. This inner voice controls a great part of your spiritual life. Listen to it carefully, for most of the time it is absolutely right.

CHAPTER 3

The Image of God

ONE OF OUR GREATEST needs is to know that we are accepted and loved by a significant other. This could be our parents, a sibling, a spouse, a close relative, or a dear friend. Each one of us has the need to feel certain, deep down in our heart, that someone loves us, cares for us, and has our best interests at heart. That is a need that God designed in us. In essence, God wants us to know that he loves every one of us with a passionate intensity too difficult to comprehend. Our part in life is to learn to love and respect ourselves as God loves us. In fact, we cannot love anybody if we do not love and respect who we really are.

In order to understand who we are in God's eyes, we must first believe in God's presence in our life. And to believe in God's presence, we need to realize that God loves us just as we are. God loves us not because we are good. No, God loves us, period. God loves us not because we are lovable. No, we are lovable precisely because God loves us. It is wonderful when we come to understand that we are unconditionally accepted, validated, and loved for who we are, apart from any of our major accomplishments or successes in our life.

Being created after the image and likeness of God (see Gen 1:26) makes human beings of infinite worth and dignity, regardless of any talent, ability, and success they may have attained. We are created by God and endowed with a particle of God, that unseen part of ourselves that keeps us alive—our soul. St. Augustine recognized this connection between the two. In spite of our failings, each feels the longing to reach out to his Creator. St. Augustine realized it is the doing of God and referred to this divine part of our human nature, seeing it as our desire to want to know God. He said, "Our hearts are restless until they find their rest in God."*

When we begin to realize that God loves us with our weakness, our vulnerability, and our failures or shortcomings, we can begin to accept them all as an inevitable part of our human life. We can be aware of our human frailties and sensitive enough that we do not impose them on other people. We can love others—with their failures—when we stop despising ourselves because of our failures. We can have compassion for ourselves and see that even our sinfulness is us acting out of our own suffering. Then, we can understand that people who do bad things or hurt others intentionally or unintentionally could be acting out of their own suffering.

God's love for us and our caring for other people are the greatest motivating forces in our life. Furthermore, this love and the good it creates will always triumph over hatred and evil. Evil may seem to win, but only for a little while; eventually it is defeated. If we wish to be in the presence of God and want to be his coworkers in transforming the world and helping the prevalence of love over selfishness—of good over evil—we must begin by understanding that as much as God loves you and me, God equally loves the whole human race.

God calls on us and sees us as his partners in working for a society where people count; where people matter more than things and more than possessions; where human life is safeguarded and respected; where people will be secure and not

---

*Augustine, *The Confessions of Saint Augustine*, bk. 1, chap. 1, trans. Rex Warner (New York: New American Library, 1963).

suffer from hunger, ignorance, or disease; where there will be more gentleness, more caring, more sharing, and more compassion; and where there is peace and joy. As St. Paul says, "Rejoice in the Lord always; again I will say, Rejoice. Let your gentleness be known to everyone. The Lord is near. Do not worry about anything, but in everything by prayer and supplication with thanksgiving let your requests be made known to God" (Phil 4:4–6).

Each and every human being is created after the image and likeness of God. The phrase "made in the image of God" refers not to the physical but to the nonphysical—the spiritual—part of our humanity. In the likeness of God, a person has a soul/spirit that sets us apart from animals and makes us just a little lower than God's other glorious creation, the angels (see Heb 2:7). Our spiritual nature enables us to commune with God and makes us like him mentally, morally, and socially. This does not mean that we are like God in the sense of being "little gods," but rather that we share in some of God's characteristics, although on a limited, finite scale. We are God's cocreators with the ability to continue the creation. This implies that we are members of God's family. We belong to him, but we are also partakers in God's plan of restoring humanity. Much work is to be done to fulfill God's plan and bring about the transformation of the suffering that exists in our world. To see each other as brothers and sisters is an enormous step toward realizing God's plan, but it does not mean that love will be without effort or that hate can be ignored. God will enable us to address this suffering from a place of love and not of hate, of forgiveness and not revenge, of humility and not arrogance, of generosity and not guilt, of courage and not fear. To be true partners with God requires seeing with the eyes of God, that is, to see with the eyes of the heart and not just with the eyes of the head.

We should not be discouraged when God's plan of salvation is delayed. There will be suffering: pain in childbirth, torment in illness, and anguish in death. Sadness, longing, and heartache do not disappear. Jesus said, "In the world you face persecution. But take courage; I have conquered the world!" (John 16:33).

In the garden of Gethsemane, Jesus could have chosen to avoid the cross and chosen to save us in a different way. The echo of his agonizing voice reaches the ears of our hearts to this day. He threw himself on the ground and prayed, "Abba, Father, for you all things are possible; remove this cup from me; yet, not what I want, but what you want" (Mark 14:36). Jesus made a deliberate choice and, in making that choice, transformed suffering that could have been a numbing, meaningless thing into something liberating and meaningful. He turned death and evil into new life and a source of good.

The experience of Jesus reminds us of our human frailty and leads us to ask, "How can we find relief and meaning in our personal suffering?" Usually, for physical injury or sickness, we search and find the right doctor to help us. With all good intentions, the doctors examine us and prescribe the right medication, and hopefully we begin to feel better. Yet most of the time, the question, "Why do I have to suffer?" still lingers in our minds.

In the Gospels of Mark and Matthew, we find a woman who had been subject to bleeding for twelve years. She had suffered a great deal under the care of many doctors and had spent all she had, but instead of getting better, she grew worse. When she heard about Jesus, she came up behind him in the crowd, touched his cloak, and said, "If I but touch his clothes, I will be made well" (Mark 5:28). Immediately, her bleeding stopped and she felt in her body that she was freed from her suffering. When Jesus asked, "Who touched my clothes?" (5:30), the woman came and fell at his feet and told him the whole truth. He said to her, "Daughter, your faith has made you well; go in peace, and be healed of your disease" (Mark 5:34).

When there is suffering in our lives, it is wise to seek

professional help. It is helpful to take the prescribed medicine, yet turning to Jesus for help can reassure us that our suffering can be transformed into a more positive experience. Ultimately, the answer is love. We take childbirth for granted. But how does a mother make her suffering of pain at childbirth into a positive thing; not an experience that makes her resentful and bitter? It is because of her love. Her pain is transformed into joy when she sees the newborn child whom she just brought to life. And that love for her child is a lasting love that follows most of us the rest of our lives.

FOR CONSIDERATION

1. God asks each of us to become aware of our qualities, to believe in them, to live them. He invites us to be ourselves and invites us to realize the positive riches he has given us. It is by means of our qualities that we establish a true relationship with God and feel his presence in our life.

2. The awareness of God's presence creates hope, optimism, motivation, and enthusiasm that can transform our lives. The presence of God is found in the depths of our heart and our qualities, gifts, and talents are expressions of God's presence.

3. Through prayer we become aware of God's presence, and we also sense it through our admiration of creation. We can say with David, "The LORD is just in all his ways, / and kind in all his doings. / The LORD is near to all who call on him, / to all

who call on him in truth. / He fulfills the desire of all who fear him…. / The LORD watches over all who love him" (Ps 145:17–20).

4. Take a moment and ask yourself the following: "What could be a desirable goal in my life? Do I want to be happy?" This is a universal desire. Then turn to God, the only source of happiness, who can take care of your needs and give you a foretaste of the life to come.

5. While life may not be the celebration we hope for, we can be assured that God will never abandon us in difficult moments. He is always present and is a friend on whom we can count in our troubled times and who responds to our needs.

CHAPTER 4

Our Quest for God

THE PSALMIST RECOGNIZES the human yearning to seek the
divine. "'Come,' my heart says, 'seek his face!' / Your face, LORD,
do I seek. / Do not hide your face from me" (Ps 27:8–9). This
yearning for the divine has been a challenge and a concern of
humankind since the beginning of creation.

We read in the Book of Genesis that God created the world
out of nothingness. The creation of the world was achieved
through the spoken word, through the successive *and God said*,
and it was so: "Then God said, 'Let there be light....Let there be
a dome in the midst of the waters....Let there be lights in the
dome of the sky to separate the day from the night....' And God
said, 'Let the earth bring forth living creatures of every kind: cat-
tle and creeping things and wild animals of the earth of every
kind.'...And God saw that it was good" (Gen 1:3–25).

The climactic point of Creation was the creation of
humankind. "Then God said, 'Let us make humankind in our
image, according to our likeness'....Male and female he created
them. God blessed them, and God said to them, 'Be fruitful and
multiply, and fill the earth and subdue it; and have dominion
over the fish of the sea and over the birds of the air and over
every living thing that moves upon the earth'" (Gen 1:26–28).

A story has been told that a scientist challenged God about
the creation of man. "Like you," the scientist said, "I can also

create a man." God responded, "Well, let me see what you can do." The scientist picked up handfuls of earth, and proudly, he began to mold a human being. "Wait a moment," God said. "You are using my earth. Go get your own earth."

The spiritual life is a life of grace that begins with an awareness that the harmony of the universe—the change of seasons, the sun that rises and sets daily with such accuracy, the moon that waxes and wanes, the stars that brighten the sky at night and all galaxies—is sustained by God's power. This awareness is increased by the belief and hope that beyond the seen physical world, there is an unseen world that is eternal.

As we look at nature, so much speaks of God's creation. For example, in autumn, the leaves of the trees begin to fall; by winter, the tree is stripped of its leaves; in springtime, the leaves gradually come back. In time, flowers appear and fruit trees bring forth fruit—God's power and providence in action.

Consider the animal kingdom, too, with its variety of creatures that exist on our planet. Then look at the creation of a human being and the billions of humans who inhabit the earth. Each of us can take a deep look into the mystery of being human. Think of our growing years, when we became aware that we were individuals with thoughts, feelings, and actions. As we review our life, the changes and transitions that we made to be where we are today, hopefully, we will arrive at the conviction that our Creator is a loving God.

Despite our sinfulness, God embraces us with love and invites us to sit at his table. He serves us with his own hands and treats us with respect as his favorites. The psalmist recognizes this wonder of God and exclaims,

> Where can I go from your spirit?
>   Or where can I flee from your presence?
> If I ascend to heaven, you are there;
>   if I make my bed in Sheol, you are there.

If I take the wings of the morning
    and settle at the farthest limits of the sea,
even there your hand shall lead me,
    and your right hand shall hold me fast.
If I say, "Surely the darkness shall cover me,
    and the light around me become night,"
even the darkness is not dark to you;
    the night is as bright as the day,
    for darkness is as light to you.

For it was you who formed my inward parts;
    you knit me together in my mother's womb.
I praise you, for I am fearfully and wonderfully made.
    Wonderful are your works;
that I know very well.
    My frame was not hidden from you,
when I was being made in secret,
    intricately woven in the depths of the earth.
Your eyes beheld my unformed substance.
In your book were written
    all the days that were formed for me,
    when none of them as yet existed.
How weighty to me are your thoughts, O God!
    How vast is the sum of them!
I try to count them—they are more than the sand;
    I come to the end—I am still with you.

                              (Ps 139:7–18)

God's wonderful creation of the world is a result of his love, of which we are all a part. Our parents, in an intimate moment of love, caused our conception. At that same moment, God gave us life. Out of love, God created us and cares for us. We are God's children and, therefore, creatures of love with an inexhaustible potential for love.

However, our quest for God takes on another dimension as we read of the fall of Adam and Eve in Genesis 3. In our daily life, if we happen to break the rules, we feel bad or uncomfortable, and sometimes try to justify or hide the violation or blame someone else. This is the experience of Adam and Eve. They hid themselves from the presence of the Lord God. The essence of the fall, not following God's command, implies the breaking of the relationship between God and them.

When we ignore or disobey divine directives, we alienate ourselves from God. A similar feeling occurs when a small disagreement begins between two people. Either we point the finger, blaming or yelling at each other, or we cease communication. Then we feel betrayed, rejected, or abandoned.

Feelings of abandonment or loneliness can only find relief when we are in good standing with God, our Creator. When we block God out of our daily life or turn to him only in dire need, God does not abandon us, because God loves us and wants to be with us in our life. Every hour of each day, God continues to care as a father cares for his children. God loves the just and shows mercy upon the sinners; he wants to be part of our lives, helping us refine our thoughts, cleanse our minds, and deliver us from all adversities, evil, and stressful situations.

As we examine our lives—our values, attitudes, and lifestyles—we may discover that we are missing the mark. We may experience unease, and guilt seeps into our psyche. Suddenly, a yearning for reconciliation surfaces in our heart. Changing direction helps us to break away from our bad attitudes and damaging habits and addictions—lying, cheating, being hypocritical, or feeling angry. We leave these behind and make some resolutions for a better future.

In the light of God's love, we can take the necessary steps to repair those damaging relationships in our life and thus restore our relationship with God. When we are faced with temptations, we invite the help of God's Spirit that abides in each of us. However, this is all the more difficult when we are in conflict with God's love, when we are angry or hate or cannot forgive someone.

Imagine if all human relationships began with the belief that people are innately wonderful and beautiful—*with an inner capacity to love*. In fact, beyond our superficiality, we are people with a potential for loving. As we come to respect the image of God in others and become part of love as the one great reality in which we can all live, we will realize that we can look *through* others instead of just *at* them; we will understand others as creatures of God with the capacity to love despite some outwardly unloving behaviors.

Consider how we deal with the people we encounter daily: our spouses, our children, our siblings, the janitor or the mail carrier, the garbage collector or the garage attendant, the taxi driver, the dentist, the receptionist, or the cashier at the supermarket. Do we see others as equals or as inferiors?

FOR CONSIDERATION

1. One of our greatest needs is to know that we are accepted and loved. Each one of us has to feel certain, deep down in our heart, that someone loves us, cares for us, and has our best interests at heart. Of equal importance is our attitude in being loving and loveable.

2. Through our parents, God gave us life. Think of God as the Giver of life and how grateful we can be for God's love and his seen and unseen blessings in our everyday life. Things that we do not have—material possessions—may not be as important as we think.

3. God wants us to know that he loves every one of us with a passionate intensity too difficult to describe. Our part in life is to learn to love ourselves as God loves us. "Love your neighbor as yourself," Jesus said. This implies that we cannot love anybody if we do not love and respect ourselves.

4. Sometimes our awareness of God's presence is darkened by arrogance, indifference, and disbelief. We may ask questions: Is there a God? Is there an afterlife? But God in his abundant mercy and goodness does not punish us for our thoughts or distorted perceptions. He continues to love us unconditionally.

5. The Lord gives us grace to offer prayers together and has promised that when two or three are gathered together in his name, he will grant their requests. "Give us this day our daily bread." The original Greek, "*Ton epiousion arton*" means, "Give us this day not simply bread but what is of essence in our life"—the wisdom and understanding of who we are in God's eyes.

CHAPTER 5

Who Is God?

GOD IS OUR CREATOR who brought us into being out of nothingness and caringly watches over us, gently leading us to our salvation and a state of inner contentment. A Greek song that I learned in third grade encapsulates God's loving care: "*Eine Theos mas odigei kai mas didaskei afta pou prepei kai rihni mia matia sti gi ki'olas tas praxis mas tas vlepei*" (It is God who guides and teaches us what we must do. He can only take a look at the earth and see all of our actions.)

God's caring love for us does not depend on us—on our mood or on our collaboration. Whether we practice our faith or not; whether we are disbelievers or unbelievers; whether we are indifferent, oblivious to his presence in our life, or fervent believers and committed to his service, we enjoy the same benefits— the gift of life, the grandeur of nature, the sun that shines, the blessing of rain, and the fruits of the earth.

God gives us life—our natural talents, our aptitudes, our energies, our dynamism, and the power to love, understand, to be free, and to have confidence. All these benefits, both known and unknown, give us a personality, a free will, a proper and distinct identity. And God continues his work by preserving what he has made—you and me—by placing at our disposal all the defense mechanisms that we need to protect ourselves against disintegration, distorted thoughts, bad behavior, premature aging, as well as the hard knocks of life and the suffering that accumulate in our interpersonal relationships—conflicting interests, jealousies, quarrels, unreasonable expectations, and negative thinking. We are truly in charge of our happiness. If we hand over the responsibility for our happiness to someone else, then we are in a false relationship that will never work, no matter how we try. Such a relationship causes trouble and heartaches. Once we believe, trust, and internalize that God is there for each one of us, our hearts thirst to find God and connect with him, and we realize that we are not alone in this life. God has made us with purpose and wants us to be happy. We are not looking for or connecting with a God who is distant or indifferent. We are seeking to find a God who loves us and is always present in our life. It is simple, yet we ask, Where do we find such a God?

If we allow God the opportunity to love us, he will guide us, sanctify us, and lead us out of our anguish, our anxieties, and our problems. He does not want to make us slaves. He wants us to be proud to be his children, without being arrogant. He wants us to walk with our heads held high, our hearts free, like someone willingly connected with an infinitely loving Father, who has freely chosen us to become his children—his sons and daughters.

God takes the responsibility for animating us, for activating us and moving us forward. He asks us to look upon him with faith and a positive attitude. We must realize that we are loved; we must let God bring about changes in us that make us better people. God wants us not to remain passive under his gaze of unconditional love. We receive many blessings from God; our part is to express our gratitude to him by being compassionate and caring for other people's needs.

We must gain the same confidence and feel inspired by what St. Paul says in his letter to the Romans:

Who will separate us from the love of Christ? Will
hardship, or distress, or persecution, or famine, or
nakedness, or peril, or sword?...No, in all these
things we are more than conquerors through him
who loved us. For I am convinced that neither death,
nor life, nor angels, nor rulers, nor things present, nor
things to come, nor powers, nor height, nor depth,
nor anything else in all creation, will be able to separate us from the love of God in Christ Jesus our Lord.
(Rom 8:35–39)

A good and positive step is to believe that you are loved by
God and to believe that God has a plan for your life, and that he
has already foreseen the means for accomplishing it—that you
have been chosen to be his instrument in the realization of this
plan. However, you must allow yourself to be possessed and
gripped by Christ without counting the cost. Through our atten-
tiveness and vigilance, we will discover God, for our attention is
the instrument that detects God. The heart of our attention is the
thought that God loves us and has done everything for us, constantly leaning over us with his presence.

When God takes hold of a heart, it suddenly becomes fas-
cinated by him and totally abandons itself into his hands. It is no
longer concerned with itself; only knowing and serving God
counts. This love of God will grow insofar as we are conscious of
what God accomplishes in us, for us, and by us, so that we may
be transformed in him as his true children. His action in us is
awesome, but it is just as beautiful in those whom we call our
neighbors. Therefore, it is up to us to discover in others this
presence of God, a presence of true friendship.

Rather than analyzing God's love with rational thinking, it
is better to accept gratefully with our hearts that he loves us

unconditionally. What is the quality of the relationship that unites us to him? It is not fear, but friendship; love, not indifference; confidence, not doubt.

Too often, we feel that God's love for us is conditional, as is our love for others. We make God in our image, thinking and acting as we do, rather than seeing ourselves in God's image. Ours is a culture of achievement, and we carry over these attitudes to our relationship with God. We work hard trying to impress everyone, including God. And yet, our relationship with God, our standing before him, has nothing to do with our work, performance, or accomplishments.

We strongly perceive within ourselves the desire not to grieve the Lord with negative thoughts and bad behavior but to accomplish all that is pleasing to him. We feel the need to meet with him in the depths of our soul when we become aware that we are God's temples, that we are truly his children and that we belong to his family. He alone is the universal author of all good and perfect gifts that he makes available to us.

Our life will be empty and boring if we ignore God's presence or if we only seek God occasionally when we are in dire need. We must become aware that God is someone alive, active, and loving—someone who lives in the heart of our being.

Reflect on a time in your life when you felt more loving, more peaceful, and more content. Perhaps you wanted to do something good for another person, or you thought of a friend and initiated a phone call. Such moments are important because you are moved by the goodness of God. This experience becomes alive in the depths of your heart, and you may want it to last. Eventually, you will rediscover those moments when the presence of God filled you with enthusiasm—those moments of spiritual euphoria. These marvelous moments appeared as a desire for more precise and conscious contact with God. It is in these moments that we are moved to pray:

Lord, teach me to be generous.
Teach me to serve you as you deserve;
to give and not to count the cost,
to fight and not to heed the wounds,
to toil and not to seek for rest,
to labor and not to ask for reward,
save that of knowing that I do your will.*

FOR CONSIDERATION

1. Imagine how God must feel at times, proud as a parent looking at us! In view of God's unconditional love for us, our
   sullen pouts, our anger, our turning away, and even such dra-
   matic outbursts, declaring, "There is no God, and if there is
   one, he does not care," look not much different to God than
   the typical three-year-old who is throwing a temper tantrum
   because Mommy is going away. God, like the mother, cannot
   help but smile. How little and silly we must appear at times.

2. We are taught that God's love is unconditional, yet seldom as
   we grow do we take that notion seriously. Our present gener-
   ation likes to believe that we have freed ourselves from some
   older fears. God was sometimes seen as someone with a big
   stick, ready to punish us for every wrong thing we did, or as

---

*St. Ignatius of Loyola, "Prayer for Generosity," http://www.bc.edu/bc_org/prs/stign/
prayers.html.

someone with a big book, recording each one of our sins to be judged after our death. Is this still your image of God?

3. Listen to the voice of Jesus and take seriously the unconditional love of God. God loves us long before any sin we commit and long after every sin we will ever commit. As a result, we can experience abundant joy in life.

4. The deepest love and respect that we can give to God, our Creator, is to thoroughly enjoy the gift of life right at this very moment. We should never take our gift of life for granted. The highest compliment someone can give to a gift giver is to enjoy the gift. The psalmist challenges us when he says, "What shall I return to the LORD / for all his bounty to me?" (Ps 116:12).

5. Remember that we are all surrounded by the presence of God, who loves us and cares for our well-being. God loves with each one of us in the deep recesses of our hearts. Enter your heart and speak into that presence with genuine gratitude for the good things you have received. Allow yourself to give thanks with joy.

Chapter 6

The Power of Faith

THERE ARE A NUMBER of occasions in the Gospels where Jesus says, "Your faith has made you well" (cf. Mark 5:34; Mark 10:52; Luke 8:48; Luke 17:19). Those afflicted with any kind of ailment, physical, emotional, or mental, became well because of their faith. The power of faith—God's gift within each person—brought about total recovery.

Through faith in Jesus and his guidance in our lives, we can overcome all things. Yet the realities of life bring distractions that can often detour us from God's path. A strong foundation of faith guides us in our daily life. Just as we need the basics—air to breathe, food to eat, water to drink, and a well-balanced lifestyle—as believers, it is important to enrich our hearts, souls, and minds with faith-based ingredients. Nurturing our spiritual health allows us to rise above daily challenges that often limit our full potential so that we can live victoriously in Christ.

In the Gospel of Luke, the disciples asked Jesus to increase their faith. Jesus replied, "If you had faith the size of a mustard seed, you could say to this mulberry tree, 'Be uprooted and planted in the sea,' and it would obey you" (Luke 17:5–6). Something great can come from something so small. Interestingly, in John's Gospel, the word *believe* appears about a hundred times, however, the word *faith* appears only a few times. For John and his community, *faith* is an active word. If they simply trusted and believed in Jesus, it would imply that they had great faith.

After his visit to different parts of Asia Minor, Greece, and Rome, St. Paul sent letters to strengthen the faith of the new believers in Christ. Notice that nowhere in his epistles did Paul tell believers to believe or to have faith. If they believed the gospel of Christ and accepted him as their Savior, they had sufficient faith.

Human faith can only trust what it can see, taste, hear, smell, or feel; it's limited to our five senses. For example, once every two years, I visit my relatives in Greece. I board an airplane, and after nine hours in the air, I arrive at my destination. In reality, I have no knowledge of how airplanes work. I know nothing about the pilot and crew, but I trust that everything will be okay, and seeing other travelers, I feel reassured; but it takes human faith and trust, which we gain as we experience air travel. Similarly, when it comes to God, we have to believe certain things that we cannot see. You and I have not seen God. As Jesus said, "Not that anyone has seen the Father except the one who is from God; he has seen the Father" (John 6:46). You and I have not seen heaven. Visually, we cannot see love or justice, sin or forgiveness, kindness or compassion. We only see their results. Can we see the air we breathe or the power of electricity? We can only experience what they mean to us.

In all these concepts, whether they are positive or negative, we believe they exist. A skeptic may ask a familiar question: "How can I believe in things I cannot see?" The answer is that human logic cannot possibly understand or believe in invisible things. St. Paul tells us we have all been given a measure of faith (see Rom 12:3), and that faith comes from God. Faith is believing in God and trusting in him regardless of the circumstances or influences around us. Sometimes we find this easy to do, but life's dilemmas can often cause our faith to weaken or fail, especially during times of sadness, loneliness, sickness, pain, depression, deprivation, or a loved one's sudden death.

When our faith is challenged, we can gain some insight as we consider the following thoughts:

1. *You were not created to worry and fret.* Worrying does not solve problems. Worry, being the absence of true faith, is the destroyer of health, wealth, and love, leaving us with bigger difficulties to worry about—all the outcomes of negative thinking. You may have heard the quote, "Worry is like a good rocking chair. It gives you something to do, but it doesn't get you anywhere." Worry will only tire you. God wants you to be at peace. "Cast your burden on the LORD, / and he will sustain you" (Ps 55:22). God not only cares for you, but he is far better at handling the weight of your problems.

2. *It can often seem easier to depend on oneself—job, friends, relatives, income, hobbies—everything except God.* Develop the habit of making God your priority, not an afterthought. Talk to him about what you really need at the very moment you need it and trust him to provide an answer. Your faith will increase as you depend more on God and less on yourself. Be patient. God may delay in responding, but he never forgets to provide an answer for the benefit of your soul.

3. *God has a plan for you and a work for you to accomplish.* Sometimes, selfishness may inadvertently move you in a different direction. He does not want you to take a wrong path that ends up in self-damage. Surrendering to God may seem unnatural at first, but his Spirit will strengthen you and guide you if you allow God to take over. Step forward in

faith to work *with* him, not *against* him. Be active in serving God by serving others.

4. *Allow your heart to hear God's message.* Our lives are frantically busy, noisy, and demanding. You must make time to listen for God's voice. In moments of prayerful stillness, the heart is encouraged and attentive. Then, with renewed faith, you are ready to move forward in obedience to the Lord's commands. "Be still, and know that I am God!" (Ps 46:10); he is ever present in your life.

5. *Patience is a profound faith builder.* We live in a world where we expect to be instantly gratified, so understandably we expect that answers to our prayers should also come promptly. However, God is not bound by time. He answers our prayers in a way that is best for us, at the time that he knows will do us the most good. We must have faith that God is working to change us from the inside, and this takes time. Be patient, and in time, he will reveal the answer to your prayer.

In addition to these thoughts, consider also your responsibilities and how you are going to participate in the process of developing your faith. First, you must be living in obedience to God—with no obstacles to your relationship. Second, when you pray to God, you must be open to his will. Third, you must be patient and wait for his timing. He knows exactly when to fulfill your wishes. Finally, remember to give thanks.

Our heavenly Father delights in hearing us give thanks. You can always find something to be thankful for. St. Paul reminds us, "Give thanks in all circumstances" (1 Thess 5:18)—not just for the good things, but in all things. Learn to give thanks even for trials and disappointments, because you never know what blessings such things can bring.

Our life here on earth is a school, and the challenges we experience each day can often be looked at as another lesson. God will always lead us into those experiences that will increase our faith, and indeed our faith will increase as we acknowledge these lessons and grow from them. Each time we pass one test, God will lovingly but certainly bring us to the next. Our choice is to use every opportunity we can to exercise our faith, and as we do, our faith will increase. Remember that Jesus is "the pioneer and perfecter of our faith" (Heb 12:2). He will not stop working with us until our faith has been perfected.

Christian faith is faith in Jesus, not in a religion. We are reminded that, "Without faith it is impossible to please God, for whoever would approach him must believe that he exists and that he rewards those who seek him" (Heb 11:6). God revealed himself in history through Jesus Christ, his Son: "He has spoken to us by a Son" (Heb 1:2). We can begin to get to know Jesus through reading about and contemplating his life, death, and resurrection in the New Testament.

FOR CONSIDERATION

1. Like most people, while we believe in Jesus, we still raise the question, "Do I have enough faith?" If we are preoccupied by our human needs and endless desires and are subject to human frailty, can we possibly have sufficient faith?

2. To answer this question—Do I have enough faith?—turn to Jesus for his response. His voice will begin to echo in your

heart: *Once you get to believe in me, to know me, and to accept me as your Savior, and sense my presence, already you have faith. If you believe my message—of love, joy, peace, unconditional acceptance of who you are, and forgiveness of your sins—you have faith.*

3. Let your heart listen to his voice. Activate and maintain a relationship with Jesus Christ—applying his teachings in your personal life—so that your faith may be revitalized and become stronger.

4. God will not abandon you in troubled times, for he has promised to never leave or forsake you. "Be content with what you have; for he has said, 'I will never leave you or forsake you'" (Heb 13:5). It is your choice to surrender to him and say to yourself with faith and confidence, "The Lord God is my helper. He knows my needs; he is in charge of my life."

5. Occasionally, you may need to sharpen your focus and understand that faith is surrendering with strong conviction and complete trust to something for which there may be no tangible proof.

PRAYER

"For everyone who asks receives, and everyone who searches finds, and for everyone who knocks, the door will be opened."

—Matthew 7:8

CHAPTER 7

God's Embrace

WE MEET GOD in the person of Jesus, who took on human form, going through all stages of development from birth to adulthood. He had a body and hungered, experienced thirst and tiredness, felt mental fatigue, frustration, and pain. He also experienced pleasure, joy, and all the bodily senses of feeling, tasting, seeing, hearing, smelling, and touching.

In the opening of the Gospel of John, we are inspired by the verse that helps our yearning to meet God: "In the beginning was the Word, and the Word was with God, and the Word was God" (John 1:1). The Word, being Christ, became flesh and dwelt among us. We, too, are flesh (*soma*) with a soul that seeks a life similar to the life of Christ. While we cannot be him, we can imitate his virtues and the life he lived among the people of his time.

Jesus' disciple Philip one day said to Jesus, "*Deixon emin ton Patera*" (Show us the Father). Jesus' reply was simple: "Have I been with you all this time, Philip, and you still do not know me? Whoever has seen me has seen the Father. How can you say, 'Show us the Father'?" (John 14:9). To see Christ is to see God.

Philip's desire to see God has been the wish and the desire of many people throughout the ages. The rewards society has offered—including money, power, sex, entertainment, and material goods—have often been distractions and hindrances to living a more meaningful, fulfilling, and spiritual life that is open to meeting God.

Many experience a feeling of being overworked and unfulfilled. Life is lived at such a frenetic pace that much of what we do—from work to family and other relationships—seems inadequate and unfulfilling. The technological innovations, including e-mail and the Internet, seem to be improved means to as-yet-unimproved ends. We seek more depth and intimacy in relationships, often because we have confused stimulation with fulfillment; nothing ever quite measures up to our expectations. If the arteries of the soul are clogged and our spiritual life suffers, how can we possibly expect to meet God?

A powerful way to meet God is to experience our place in the biblical stories by imagining ourselves as characters in the time of Jesus. The Gospels are great places to begin. As a start, let me suggest the familiar story of the prodigal son.

The prodigal son took the wrong path, which led him into darkness. Ignoring parental care and love, he took his part of the inheritance and went to another country to live. There, in loose living, he wasted all that he owned and became hungry and lost. Somehow, sometimes, some of us see ourselves as present-day prodigal sons or daughters. We waste God's gifts of joy, peace, love, and freedom, ignoring his abundant blessings and walking lonely in the darkness while wasting our precious life.

There are times when I have distanced myself from God and my faith. After experiencing spiritual hunger and inner emptiness, I eventually return to my senses, I recall the prodigal son's father—how he accepted unconditionally his straying son and prepared a big celebration for his return.

It is then that I think of God, our compassionate Father, waiting for my return. My thoughts about his unconditional love bring me back to my senses and give me the courage to come back and be near him. Once I begin my return home to God's love, I wrestle with my passive procrastination and resistances. Within me, I sense a strange feeling of pride, leading me away from God, weakening me and causing despair. I have an opportunity to prepare myself for genuine repentance.

Finally, the conflicts and the unseen warfare within me stop. I know that God was already waiting for my return. How did I know? Because his compassion became real to me as I recalled the words of the prophet Ezekiel: God does not wish the death of a sinner. Rather, he expects him to return as a repentant (see 33:11). All of us have experienced a sense of guilt. Guilt creates passivity and stifles growth, maturity, and the potential of happiness.

If at any time in your life you have felt distanced from God or you became a disbeliever, whatever discomfort you feel at this reading—emotional, physical, or spiritual—take this opportunity to turn and meet God, our loving Father. Pause for a couple of seconds, close your eyes, and take three deep breaths. Air is God's gift of life that you inhale. Just relax and cherish the moment. Then start reading slowly the following prayer:

> Heavenly Father, as the prodigal son came back to his father's house and his father welcomed him, embraced and kissed him, likewise I am coming back and beg You, Lord.
> I have sinned against You.
> Have mercy upon me and forgive my wrongs and unwitting errors.
> I acknowledge my voluntary and involuntary sins.
> Genuinely, I admit that I am guilty.
> But I'm back under Your grace, not as a slave of my passions but as a free person.
> I am starving for your Fatherly acceptance and love.
> Please feed my soul with Your precious presence.

Fill my life with the fruits of the Holy Spirit—love, joy,
   peace, patience, kindness, generosity, faithfulness,
   gentleness, and self-control.
I know that in Your unfathomable love, You will accept
   me and embrace me as one of your sons or as one of
   your daughters,
who at last came to his or her senses and now needs the
   kiss of forgiveness. Amen.

Most of us are like the prodigal son. Eventually, we become
aware of our wrongdoings—anger, negative thoughts, judging
others, inability to forgive someone who did us wrong, and com-
plaints. However, as we respond to the call of our conscience, we
arise and go to our Father. The Father in his compassion
stretches out his arms to welcome us, forgive us, embrace us,
and kiss us.

Let's look again at our story. The young man takes the first
step. He comes to his senses, overcomes his blindness, and sees
what he must do. Before he ever gets out of the pigpen, he admits
his sinfulness, as he says to himself, "I will get up and go to my
father, and I will say to him, 'Father, I have sinned against heaven
and before you; I am no longer worthy to be called your son;
treat me like one of your hired hands'" (Luke 15:18–19). Some
people may find it difficult to believe the meaning of the story
because of our human condition. The father welcomes the son
back instantly—he doesn't even wait for him to get to the house.
"Quickly…" says the father, "get the fatted calf and kill it, and let
us eat and celebrate; for this son of mine was dead and is alive
again; he was lost and is found!" (15:22–24). Celebration makes
sense only when there is really something to celebrate.

In this parable, it is imperative to notice the concept of reconciliation. Look how Jesus portrays our heavenly Father in this
parable. The father, seeing his son in the distance, *runs out to meet
him.* An older man running in that part of the world would rarely

have happened, but Jesus used that expression to emphasize the love of our heavenly Father, who anticipates our return. The father of this story not only runs out to meet his son, he also embraces and kisses him: "*Katefilisen afton*" (He kissed him over and over).

Through one loving gesture, the father forgives the son—and the son hasn't even made his confession yet! When he does, it seems the father hardly listens. The confession is not the most important thing here; the important thing is that his son has returned. The son need not beg for forgiveness; he has already been forgiven. This is the glorious good news: God's mercy and forgiveness, like God's love, do not stop. Jesus reveals to us a loving God who can simply forgive! God really is like the merciful parent in this parable: not out to catch us in our sin and punish us, but reaching, in spite of our sin and the wrong we did, to bring us back to him, where there is abundant love.

FOR CONSIDERATION

1. Jesus is not merely a historical personality but someone who is alive today and presently working to accomplish his purposes of saving people and preparing them for the kingdom of God. Do you want to know Jesus and have a relationship with him? It is possible to know him personally, although he is no longer physically present in the world. He already knows us personally, and he desires for us to know him personally as well.

2. Jesus is present in the New Testament. In fact, he is more present today than ever before! Because he is present, it is

possible to know him, to hear his voice, and to have a personal relationship with him.

3. During his earthly ministry, Jesus, God made man, walked on the earth and could only be in one place at a time as a human being. Although in his divine nature he was able to work great miracles, he was limited as a human. But now that Jesus has risen from the dead and ascended into heaven, all that has changed! Today, Jesus is present not just in one place at a time, but in all places where believers are present (see Matt 18:20).

4. St. Paul tells us that we are the body of Christ, and every one of us possesses a gift and is called to use it in service to continue Christ's teaching and healing ministry. Today, you and I are his hands and feet sent out to accomplish his purposes in the world (see 1 Cor 12), working in every believer through the Holy Spirit to help and relieve people from suffering and to show them a new way of life. Jesus is present through us, here and now. He is always with us, for he tells us, "I am with you always, to the end of the age" (Matt 28:20).

5. Whenever believers gather together in fellowship, Jesus joins with them through the Spirit. "For where two or three are gathered in my name, I am there among them" (Matt 18:20). Paul also tells us that "God chose to make known how great among the Gentiles are the riches of the glory of this mystery, which is Christ in you, the hope of glory" (Col 1:27). Jesus is no longer with us as a physical being but as a spiritual one, ever abiding in our hearts.

6. Pause for a few seconds, and as you place your right hand on your heart, say,

Lord and Master of my life,
Deliver me from a passive spirit,
from ambition, meddling and
    idle talk.
Give me, Your servant,
the spirit of prudence, humility,
    patience and love.
Yes, Lord and King, grant that
I may see my wrongs and faults,
and not to judge my brother
    or sister.
For You are blessed for ever.
Amen.

—*Saint Ephraim the Syrian*

CHAPTER 8

The Good News

PROPHETS FORETOLD HIS coming, angels announced his birth, wise men from the East brought him gifts: gold for his kingliness, frankincense for his heavenly origin, and myrrh, a symbol of sorrow and healing. From this beginning, the divine and human personality of God's own Son entered our earthly life. His life, death, resurrection, and ascension have affected human lives for the last two thousand years. His life on earth was marked by the miracles he performed, the stories and parables that he told, and the message of love and forgiveness that he conveyed. He healed the sick, comforted the afflicted, broke bread with the poor, and ate with the rich.

The four Gospels tell us everything about our Lord Jesus Christ, God in human form. For three years, his disciples followed him, listened to his message, witnessed his many miracles, and experienced his tragic sentence of death by crucifixion. Upon his resurrection, Jesus Christ appeared to his disciples, spoke to them, and broke bread with them. At the time of his ascension, they heard his final command: "Go therefore and make disciples of all nations, baptizing them in the name of the Father and of the Son and of the Holy Spirit, and teaching them to obey everything that I have commanded you. And remember, I am with you always, to the end of the age" (Matt 28:19–20).

Touched by God in human form and convinced who the

true God really is, the disciples went out to different nations and proclaimed the good news everywhere. They recalled and believed these words of their Lord. They felt his presence in their lives, confirming their message.

The echo of his voice has resonated in the hearts of devout personalities—great fathers, heroes of faith, and saints—who have made known to the world the good news of the loving God who is present in our lives. Furthermore, the good news is that we have a loving God who cares for his people, accepting and wanting them to have a happy and rewarding life. His unconditional love is expressed through his coming into our world in person. In order that we might understand his love, God became human in Jesus Christ, whose unique mission was to love, to forgive, to heal, and to save the people from their sins and restore the image and likeness of God in them. This signified the birth of new hope for all people, and the promise of eternal life to all who believe that our Lord and Savior Jesus Christ truly is the Son of God.

The Acts of the Apostles tells us of the beginnings of the Christian church and, as such, is the historical link that joins the life of Christ with the growth of the Christian church. It presents a condensed history—not an exhaustive story. The author, presumably Luke, includes essential details from the earliest days of the Christian movement. Besides showing that the Christian faith is firmly rooted in the facts of history, Acts teaches us about the worldwide mission of the Christian church. This worldwide mission is found in the first chapter: "You will receive power when the Holy Spirit has come upon you; and you will be my witnesses in Jerusalem, in all Judea and Samaria, and to the ends of the earth" (Acts 1:8). The phrase "to the ends of the earth" tells us that what started in Jerusalem will one day reach to the farthest corners of the globe. That was Jesus' plan from the beginning—that the good news would go in every direction and be for everyone.

In fourth-century Constantinople, present-day Istanbul, emerged one of the greatest of the early church fathers, whose deep faith and eloquence awarded him the name Chrysostom—golden-mouth—(347–407). With the ears of faith, the following vignette from one of his homilies shakes us into realization of the love of God for us, each of whom is indeed the sinful woman:

> God desired a harlot, and how does He act? He does not send to her any of His angels or archangels. No, He Himself draws near to the one He loves. He does not bring her to Heaven, but He comes down to earth, to the harlot, and is not ashamed. He visits her secret house and finds her in her drunkenness. And how does He come? Not in the bare essence of His original nature, but in the guise of one whom the harlot is seeking, in order that she might not be afraid when she sees Him, and will not run away to escape Him. He comes to the harlot as a man. And how does he do this? He is conceived in the womb, He grows little by little, as we do in a human body that she may understand Him. He finds this harlot thick with sores and oppressed by the devils. How does He react? He draws near her. Afraid as she sees Him, she is about to run away. He calls her back saying, "Why are you afraid? I am not a judge, but a physician. I come not to judge you but to save you." She comes back and is transformed. He takes her and espouses her to Himself, and gives her the signet-ring of the Holy Spirit, as a seal between them.*

This metaphor is one of the most convincing statements of God's unconditional love for a corrupt and disturbed society. It

---

*John Chrysostom, "Homily II on Eutropius," no. 11.

is also a personal reassurance to a fallen human being who considers himself or herself sinful and unworthy. God's response of love is different from our human perceptions.

Fifteen centuries later, we go to the Greek island of Crete, and there we meet one of the most prolific writers in Greek history, Nikos Kazantzakis (1883–1954). In his portrait of Zorba, a lover of life, with a touch of humor, Kazantzakis captures this loving and forgiving God when he says,

> I think of God as being exactly like me, only bigger, stronger, crazier, and immortal. He's sitting on a pile of soft sheepskins, and his hut's the sky. In his right hand he's holding not a knife or a pair of scales—those damned instruments are meant for butchers and grocers—no, he's holding a large sponge full of water, like a rain cloud. Paradise is on his right, Hell is on his left. Here comes a soul; the poor little thing's quite naked, because it's lost its cloak—its body, I mean—and it's shivering. The naked soul throws itself at God's feet. "Mercy!" it cries. "I have sinned." And away it goes reciting its sins. It recites a whole rigmarole and there's no end to it. God thinks this is too much. He yawns. "For heaven's sake, stop!" he shouts. "I've heard enough of all that!" Flap! Slap! a wipe of the sponge, and he washes out all the sins. "Away with you, clear out, run off to Paradise!" he says to the soul, because God, you know, is a great lord, and that's what being a lord means: to forgive!*

A novelist may use poetic license to make a story interesting. Kazantzakis simply offers his perception of God's love.

---

*Nikos Kazantzakis, *Zorba the Greek*, trans. Peter Bien (New York: Simon and Schuster, 2014), 105.

Reconciliation is not just a matter of getting rid of sin or feeling forgiven. It is rather the realization that God's infinite mercy permeates and heals our ailing souls. Reconciliation is often a long, sometimes painful process. Admitting our sins is one aspect of the process. It is actually the external expression of the interior transformation that change of mind has brought about in us. "Confess your sins to one another, and pray for one another, so that you may be healed" (Jas 5:16). Confession implies disclosing and acknowledging something damaging or discomforting to oneself. It also means revealing one's wrongdoing to God, to a priest, to a minister of the church, or to a spiritual counselor. As we admit and divulge our guilt, we regain relief and peace of mind. It is an adventurous journey inundated with challenges and choices, but through this process, we become participants in God's kingdom.

Why confess one's sins? And why confess to a priest or to anyone? Why not confess directly to God, since God has already forgiven me anyway? From God's perspective, there is no need. However, as human beings who do not live in our minds alone, we firstly need to externalize bodily—with words, signs, and gestures—what is in our minds and hearts. We need to see, hear, and feel forgiveness—not just think about it. We need other human beings to help us externalize what is within and open our hearts before the Lord. Confessors are not faceless and impersonal judges but guides in our discernment, compassionately helping us experience and proclaim the mercy of God in our life. God's offer of unconditional forgiveness to anyone, any sinner who comes to him, makes us feel good psychologically. Second, in the face of such love and forgiveness, we may feel uncomfortable. How can God ever forgive me? It creates a pressure within us that makes us feel that we should "do something" to deserve such largess—or at least feel a little bit guilty or even feel the need to be punished.

If we have not been loved in our growing years by our parents or significant others and have not learned how to love, it can be hard for us to perceive God's love. All we need is to hear Christ's words to the thief who had acknowledged his sinful life: "Truly I tell you, today you will be with me in Paradise" (Luke 23:43).

FOR CONSIDERATION

1. As you consider this chapter, write your insights about your perception of God. Start with your gratitude for the beautiful gifts that have been showered upon you in the course of your life. Whatever blessing or gift you have had, who has been the generous giver?

2. As you listen to the voice of God's Spirit that abides in your heart, hear that you are a precious and cherished person, among many other wonderful people. Listen carefully and try to understand that other people search and struggle like you and also wonder if God really loves them.

3. It is often difficult to remember that God loves us and understands our situation. He loves us not because we are so good. No, he loves us, period. He loves us not because we are lovable. No, we are lovable precisely because God loves us.

4. God's love, which has created and sustains us, knows our limits as well as our potential, our capacity for doing good or evil, and our tendency to be self-centered and exploit others

or our own needs. Yet God's love does not seek to confine or manipulate us. Instead, it offers us the constant grace of self-knowledge and acceptance that can liberate us to recognize a larger love.

5. It is liberating, heartwarming, and marvelous when we come to understand that we are accepted for who we are, apart from any achievement or any effort to gain God's approval. Each one of us is loved with an everlasting love, because we are the favored children of a loving Creator.

CHAPTER 9

God's Invitation

A RELATIONSHIP WITH GOD is easy if we are in touch with our own humanness and know and accept who we really are. This involves appreciating the mystery of being human—how we came into this world—and respecting and loving our life. Once we place ourselves in the presence of God, our relationship with him is at work.

How do we begin a relationship with God? Do we wait for a terminal illness or an earthquake or lightning to strike? Do we devote ourselves to charitable causes? Do we join a mission to serve the indigenous in an undeveloped country? While many of these noble efforts give us a feeling of importance, they do not necessarily establish a relationship with God.

Once we begin to believe in the presence of God and become convinced of it, our hearts begin to hunger to *find* God in our life. Once our appetite is whetted, we desire to find God in a much different way than looking for a new car, bigger house, or major accomplishment. What we really desire is *intimacy* with God; we want to be *connected* and in good standing with God.

How can we connect with God? Another question is who are we connecting with? God made us with a *purpose*—to be happy and in God's presence forever. We are not looking for or connecting with a God who is distant or indifferent. Our God is passionately engaged in drawing us to the fullness of life for which we were created. We are seeking to find a God who *loves us* and is always seeking intimacy with us. It is simple. A sense of *absence* vanishes when we are open to a sense of *presence*.

St. Basil, another church father of the fourth century, confirms our relationship with God in this prayer:

> Lord, lover of humans, out of your love you created man and woman and honored them with your own image and likeness. You placed them in Paradise, promising life eternal and the enjoyment of good things in keeping your commandments. But when they disobeyed you, the true God, you banished them from Paradise. Yet in the midst of their corrupted life, you did not turn yourself away from them, but in different times through compassion and mercy you visited them, one generation after another. You spoke to them through the mouths of prophets and holy people, challenging their wrongdoings, guiding and pointing them the way to their salvation. And when the fullness of time came, you spoke to us by your Son. Although He was God from the beginning, in time He appeared on earth, taking on the human form—teaching, forgiving, and healing—to restore humans to their original glory. He finally gave up His life to redeem people of their sins and transgressions.*

It is with faith, respect, and humility that we can meditate upon these words of wisdom. As we make them our personal spiritual property, they will open up new horizons for us, and bring us closer to the Giver of all good things.

While God is infinite, he desires to meet us and is very personal and intimate in his relationship with us. Those who live in

*From the Divine Liturgy of St. Basil the Great (4th Century).

intimacy with God are sometimes granted favors and blessed with certain privileges and gifts, such as inspiration, the power of healing, and a desire to do good for others. These gifts are like lights in the darkness to confirm his presence among his people and to rekindle spiritual awareness and faith. Jesus reassures us of God's presence when he says, "The kingdom of God is within you" (Luke 17:21 KJV). In other words, enter your heart, seek more eagerly, and you will find the riches of heaven. Outside of you is death, and the door to death is sin. Within you—in your heart—there is God.

The next step is to keep your heart pure—not the organ that pumps blood through the body, but the unseen storehouse of emotions and feelings. "Create in me a clean heart, O God, and put a new and right spirit within me," cried King David when the prophet Nathan brought him into realization that he had committed two grave sins: adultery and murder. Once the king looked inward, what did he find in his heart? Passions, power, lust, hardness, coldness of heart that desired to do whatever felt good for his own flesh. Acknowledging his crime, he turned to God with a penitent spirit and a humble heart, and said,

> I know my transgressions,
>   and my sin is ever before me.
> Against you, you alone, have I sinned,
>   and done what is evil in your sight....
>
> Therefore teach me wisdom in my secret heart.
> Purge me with hyssop, and I shall be clean;
>   wash me, and I shall be whiter than snow.
>
> (Ps 51:3–7)

Throughout the Book of Psalms, King David's transformation is evident. He made strenuous efforts to control his thoughts and the dispositions of his heart. And when he felt forgiven and reconciled with God, he said, "I have calmed and quieted my soul, / like a weaned child with its mother; / my soul is like the weaned child that is with me" (Ps 131:2).

In Psalm 34, we read that God "is near to the broken-hearted, / and saves the crushed in spirit" (34:18). God does not promise a problem-free life, but he does give peace and strength to those who accept him. For a new beginning, open your heart to God's love and plan for you.

Now, sometimes we ignore or disobey God's command-ments, we do not listen to his message, and we do things our way. In fact, St. Paul reminds us that we "all have sinned and fall short of the glory of God" (Rom 3:23), and later he says that "the wages of sin is death" (6:23)—spiritual separation from God. However, the good news is that God sent his Son into the world to bring joy and peace, to reveal the power of his love, which saves people from their sins. Christ offered his life on the cross to pay the penalty of our sins. Jesus died in our place so that we could live with him in eternity. "God so loved the world that he gave his only Son, so that everyone who believes in him may not perish but may have eternal life" (John 3:16).

When you pray and request to have a relationship with Jesus, your request is unconditionally accepted. Jesus promised that he would enter our lives, if we ask him. As the Book of Revelation reminds us, "Listen! I am standing at the door, knock-ing; if you hear my voice and open the door, I will come in to you and eat with you, and you with me" (Rev 3:20). It is with this confidence that we can approach God, "That if we ask any-thing according to his will, he hears us" (1 John 5:14).

God has made it possible for us to have a relationship with him. And we come to him based on what he did for us, rather than what we can do. During his earthly life, Jesus went to great lengths to bring us into relationship with God. Jesus spoke the truth, healed the sick, brought dead people back to life, and showed forgiveness, unconditional acceptance, and love to sinners. But most importantly, as St. Peter makes clear, "Christ also suffered for sins once for all, the righteous for the unrighteous, in order to bring you to God" (1 Pet 3:18).

When people invite Jesus into their life, it is exciting to know that their feelings change to joy, having attained a true relationship with God. They are at peace with God: "Therefore, since we are justified by faith, we have peace with God through our Lord Jesus Christ" (Rom 5:1).

FOR CONSIDERATION

1. To grow in our relationship with God and get to know God better, we need to spend time in getting to know Jesus in the Gospels and applying the teachings of Jesus Christ as recorded in the New Testament.

2. A good way to start a relationship with Jesus Christ is to start reading the Gospels of Mark or Luke. Of course, you may continue reading the Acts of the Apostles, which is a most inspirational book and tells the beginnings of the Christian church and how the teachings of Christ began to permeate the world.

3. God expresses himself through his creation. He speaks through the scriptures, through the prophets, through holy and humble people, through all that is pure. Like a friend, he is present in the actions and daily blessings that he bestows

upon the world. Listen to the mystical voice with the ears of your soul.

4. God is the source of all that exists. He is the most loving One to whom all of us belong, upon whom all of us depend, and to whom all of us wish to belong. While God can never be understood, the believer who feels God's presence and greatness becomes ecstatic in wonder, love, and praise.

5. Reflect on the following passage: "As the Father has loved me, so I have loved you; abide in my love. If you keep my commandments, you will abide in my love, just as I have kept my Father's commandments and abide in his love. I have said these things to you so that my joy may be in you, and that your joy may be complete" (John 15:9–11).

CHAPTER 10

When God Seems Distant

HAVING GOD IN OUR LIFE is potentially the most exciting, fulfilling, and significant experience. Often when we feel cut off from God, it is because of our preoccupation with worldly events, things we want to do that pull us away—fantasies, dreams, and aspirations. Understandably, our busy lives, our concerns about being healthy and happy, emotionally secure and financially stable, tend to be our priorities. We have expectations of ourselves and of others, and we want things done in a certain way—*our way*—and if we don't get what we want, we become disappointed.

I recall a story about a middle-aged couple who were traveling by car on their way for vacation. They were very excited and began to recall when vacations were their most desired annual event. Suddenly, the wife moved a little closer to her husband, and in a romantic tone she whispered, "Remember how we always used to sit so close together as you were driving and even held hands? Now look how far we sit from each other." The husband, after a few seconds of silence, smiled and said, "Honey, I have always sat at this end, driving, but look at you. You tend to sit far at the other end of the passenger's seat. It feels good when you sit closer to me."

The inference of the story reminds us that God has always been in his place, in charge of the world and indifferent as to where we are, so we distance ourselves. Distancing ourselves from God indicates a major spiritual problem. Let's briefly face what in reality happens often in our lives, and then we can indulge ourselves in some much-needed reassurance and inspiration.

Many people have had some form of religious experience—attended church frequently, joined prayer meetings, visited a shrine, or participated in a charitable project—and yet they do not have a real sense of a spiritual life. Many people convince themselves that they are devout Christians—looking like true believers, behaving like good citizens—and yet have not understood what it means to be spiritual people. Our intention is not to judge these people or accuse them of being indifferent to a spiritual life. In reality, we don't know their true thoughts and feelings about God.

As we have noted earlier, each of us is important to God. His word guarantees that if we are willing to give up our wrong or negative attitudes and ask for direction, trusting that Jesus died for the sins of the whole world, then God's forgiveness is unconditionally ours. Furthermore, if we have his understanding and forgiveness, we have full access to God. Even with our human feelings—whether we feel guilty, depressed, sick, or foolish—God still loves us, for he is a compassionate and loving God.

God longs to save us from any sort of suffering. In Jesus, God has taken the initiative, and what he has started, he will complete. If we honestly ask God to forgive us, then we are forgiven, unless we doubt his love and stubbornly insist on feeling guilty. The fact remains that we need God's forgiveness to regain peace of mind.

If you are seeking God's love, you will find it. If you want God's forgiveness, you will have it. That's the divine promise. Just keep knocking on God's door and it shall be opened to you. The slight tinge of your spiritual longing is proof that God is actively working in your life. As the Gospel of John says, "No one can come to me unless drawn by the Father who sent me" (John 6:44), and St. Paul adds, "For it is God who is at work in you, enabling you both to will and to work for his good pleasure" (Phil 2:13).

The divine commitment is not that we will *feel* that God is close, but that he *will* be close. Our new spiritual experiences are strengthened through prayers that come from our hearts. It will take time for the results to become obvious. When we give our life to Christ, we gain the most wonderful and most powerful friend in the entire universe. However, we also gain a fearsome foe. He is, in a way beyond our imagination, a powerful and evil genius, subtly appearing disguised as an interesting influence. But with God on our side, we have what it takes to overcome these negative influences. The most common of these influences is the feeling of doubt. We are reminded of the temptations of Jesus, when Satan tried putting doubts in Jesus' mind after he had fasted forty days and forty nights and was hungry.

> The tempter came and said to him, "If you are the Son of God, command these stones to become loaves of bread." But he answered, "It is written,
>
> 'One does not live by bread alone,
>   but by every word that comes from the mouth of
>   God.'"
>
> Then the devil took him to the holy city and placed him on the pinnacle of the temple, saying to him, "If you are the Son of God, throw yourself down; for it is written,
>
> 'He will command his angels concerning you,'
>   and 'On their hands they will bear you up,
> so that you will not dash your foot against a stone.'"

Jesus said to him, "Again it is written, 'Do not put the Lord your God to the test.'"

Again, the devil took him to a very high mountain and showed him all the kingdoms of the world and their splendor; and he said to him, "All these I will give you, if you will fall down and worship me." Jesus said to him, "Away with you, Satan! for it is written,

'Worship the Lord your God,
  and serve only him.'"

Then the devil left him, and suddenly angels came and waited on him. (Matt 4:3–11)

It is more than likely that we will also encounter the tempter, who uses mental disturbances or other means to tempt us. He could possibly give us a false spiritual experience. Temptations start with doubts: "Is there such a thing as God? If there is a God, how come he allows bad things to happen—accidents, earthquakes, floods, wars, and deaths of innocent people?" Such questions have no logical answer and only serve to raise doubts in our minds. In these moments of doubt, it is good to heed the advice of St. James: "Submit yourselves therefore to God. Resist the devil, and he will flee from you" (Jas 4:7).

From a human point of view, God has created a world that is less than perfect—or else it would be heaven—and in which suffering, disease, and pain are realities. Some of these we create for ourselves and blame God. Rather than become over-worried about your doubts, start with what you *do* believe, and draw strength from God, who gives us strength to endure adversity. God's power within us enables us to face the difficult times in our life. God is always present in our life, and he is caring and powerful. We can forget any deficiency that we sense within our human nature and remember instead the sufficiency of Christ's gift within each of us, which is the Holy Spirit.

It remains true that God must take some responsibility for the world in which we live. He permits evil things to take place, but he also gives us the power to combat critical issues, wherein we exercise our free will to make the world the best we can. By virtue of our choices, we can improve upon it or leave it impoverished. In this less than perfect world, our free will, as we know from personal and social experiences, can be a mixed blessing in what it bestows on us. Free will is such a critical gift for humanity. We could use it constructively to benefit ourselves and others, or we could use it in a destructive way that would deprive us of a good life. Furthermore, using our free will destructively turns our world into a living hell and leads us away from God's power, or more precisely, away from how God could exercise that power in the world.

Faith is a gift and cannot be controlled by us. We must continually look to God to strengthen our faith. No one has perfect faith. Sometimes, even the greatest believers waver in their faith, which is not a nonstop flight above reality; it's a fight. What distinguishes people of faith is not how often they hit the dirt, but how often they get up again. When hit hard by life's negative experiences—betrayal, death, divorce, unemployment, rebellious children—we can all find ourselves questioning God's existence, mercy, love, or ability and willingness to help. It is helpful to approach this in the right way—by bringing our doubts into the open.

Very young infants don't ask questions. They just accept everything around them quite happily, unless they are uncomfortable. But four-year-olds are totally different! They ask endless questions. How? When? Where? Why? Who? They have become more mentally aware of the world around them, and are trying to make sense of it all and understand how it all fits together. If they ask, "Why did you do that, Mommy?" it is not because they doubt their mother's love or wisdom. More often, they are trying to understand how her actions fit into the general scheme of things. They are on a steep learning curve.

Spiritually, we are all on a steep learning curve also, and so were the disciples of Jesus. At the Last Supper, Jesus said, "I still have many things to say to you, but you cannot bear them now" (John 16:12). You have faith—maybe not as strong as you would like, but you have it. And Jesus taught that as you use what you have, God will give you more (see Luke 16:10; Matt 25:21). If we had to become perfect—whether you define that as having absolute faith, giving up every sin, being absolutely sincere, or whatever—no one would ever be saved. You are not asked to believe that *you* are good, lovable, or dependable. You just have to believe that *God* is good, lovable, and dependable. Having faith sufficient to receive God's blessings is fully within your grasp. God's word affirms that he is our God and he loves us, regardless of how abandoned, unloved, and insignificant we may think we are. That makes spiritual success inevitable.

So often, God seems to overlook us deliberately. So often, the Bible seems as dry as dust. So often, we feel as if we have nothing to live for. Our emotional pain seems endless. God constantly seems to favor others over us. But *nothing* can change the constancy of the enormity of God's love. Nothing can make God break his word. We can sense that God is closer than we could ever imagine by creating a family and a community where all people can realize their potential to live lives worthy of their calling to be faithful, hopeful, and loving. Stop doubting long enough to receive your rightful inheritance!

FOR CONSIDERATION

1. For some people who are just starting to explore a spiritual life, it is perfectly normal that they feel nothing at first. After a while, they will receive more and more evidence that God is not far away, but such awareness takes time. Like the growth of a tree, much of God's work is not immediately obvious.

2. Every time we do something, our soul trusts the integrity of God. When we sit on a chair, for instance, we trust that God won't suddenly change the laws of physics and let us crash to the floor. Christian faith is trusting in the Creator's dependability and closeness to us.

3. Regardless of our beliefs or perceptions about God, he loves us and wants us to live out the virtues of love, hope, and faith (see 1 Cor 13). Furthermore, he wants each one of us to embody in all that we do the fruits of the Spirit: love, joy, peace, patience, kindness, generosity, faithfulness, gentleness, and self-control (Gal 5:22–23).

4. Whenever God seems distant, it is wise to heed the words of the psalmist, "Search me, O God, and know my heart; / test me and know my thoughts. / See if there is any wicked way in me, / and lead me in the way everlasting" (Ps 139:23–24). "Teach me the way I should go, / for to you I lift up my soul"

(Ps 143:8). Be patient and know that God will reveal the way that you must take.

5. Often, we wrongly think our faith seems to be so insignificant that we don't bother using it. To achieve great things in God, simply use the faith you already have. Take your eyes off the supposed inadequacy in your faith and turn them to the adequacy of God's presence. He is all we need.

CHAPTER 11

When God Seems Absent

THE CROSS IS A paradox that not only presents death but brings hope. It provides comfort and challenges our rational thinking. While in the presence of Jesus Christ, we cherish his abundant blessings and unconditional love, but there sometimes appears the presence of evil, whose destiny is to destroy. In the case of Christ, we notice mental agony, physical pain, torturous death, and crucifixion. But after the agonizing pain of Good Friday came the joy of resurrection.

Any time you sense the absence of God in your life, remember Jesus on the cross. In his human nature, Jesus felt abandoned and lonely. Hanging naked on the cross, mocked, and breathing his last breath, he cried, "My God, my God, why have you forsaken me?" (Matt 27:46).

God, where are you when I need you most? is the silent cry of people of all ages who, during some difficult time in their lives, have felt rejected or abandoned. We need to remind ourselves that God did not abandon his Son. Although the scene at Golgotha seemed the most godforsaken place on earth, God did not abandon Jesus. Neither will God abandon you or me, for we are his children whom he brought into life out of love.

William Paul Young describes the story of Mackenzie, also known as Mack, in his novel *The Shack*. Mackenzie's youngest daughter, Missy, has been abducted during a family vacation, and evidence that she may have been brutally murdered is found in an abandoned shack deep in the Oregon wilderness. Four years later, in the midst of his great sadness, Mack receives a suspicious note, apparently from God, inviting him back to that shack for a weekend. Against his better judgment, he arrives at the shack on a wintry afternoon, and there he experiences a shocking confrontation with God, represented by three human beings, implying the Trinity. A wave of emotions, a mixture of anger and longings, washes over Mack. *Is one of these God or the killer of my daughter?* he thinks.

The Shack's depiction of God as Papa is an interesting portrait that isn't meant to be taken literally as much as to capture many of the attributes of God that we read about in the Bible. These characters' interactions with Mack show that God is compassionate and loving, and that he desires a close relationship with each of us. The interactions give us a better understanding of some aspects of God's nature. God relates to us in the ways that we will best be able to hear him. Consider, for example, the following encounter between Papa and Mack:

> Mack just stood there puzzled, not knowing what to say.
>
> "Only I can set you free, Mack, but freedom can never be forced," Papa said, seeing agony in his eyes.
>
> "How can you really know how I feel?" Mack asked.
>
> …Papa didn't answer….Mack noticed the deep scars on [Papa's] wrists, like those he now assumed Jesus also had on his….Tears were slowly making their way down [Papa's] face…."Don't you ever think that what my son chose to do didn't cost us dearly? Love always leaves a significant mark….We were there *together*."
>
> Mack was surprised. "At the cross?" "Now wait, I thought you *left* him—you know—'My God, my God,

why hast thou forsaken me?'" It was a Scripture that had often haunted Mack....

"You misunderstand the mystery there. Regardless of what he *felt* at that moment, I never left him."

"How can you say that? You abandoned him just like you abandoned me!"

"Mackenzie, I never left him, and I have never left you."

"That makes no sense to me," he snapped.

"I know it doesn't, at least not yet. Will you at least consider this: When all you can see is your pain, perhaps then you lose sight of me?..."

..."Mack, don't forget, the story didn't end in his sense of forsakenness. He found his way through it to put himself completely into my hands. Oh, what a moment that was!"*

As a myth, the story gives significant evidence of God's presence. The author of *The Shack* is not a theologian and does not mention the fact that after the crucifixion, the resurrection took place. The reality of the resurrection hardly enters our minds when our agonizing souls raise the question, "Where is God when I need him most?" I recall my oldest daughter, Mersene, who had asked me that same question when the tragedy of September 11, 2001, happened. "Dad, why didn't God stop those terrorists?"

"I wish I could answer you rationally," I said. "But I derive comfort from my faith that reassures me that Christ was there, receiving the unfortunate victims as they were passing through the dark valley of death, comforting their grieving spouses, parents, siblings, relatives, and friends and strengthening those

---

*Wm. Paul Young, *The Shack* (Newbury Park, CA: Windblown Media, 2011), 95–96.

brave people who, at the risk of their own lives, made heroic efforts to help." As I thought of Christ, once again, I visualized him on the cross. When tragedies occur in our lives, Christ is recrucified, sharing our pain, always leaving us with the promise, "Take courage; I have conquered the world," meaning that after the cross, which most of us seem to bear, resurrection and new life are to come.

The question of God's absence is echoed in the psalmist:

How long, O LORD? Will you forget me forever?
　　How long will you hide your face from me?
How long must I bear pain in my soul,
　　and have sorrow in my heart all day long?...

But I trusted in your steadfast love;
　　my heart shall rejoice in your salvation.
I will sing to the LORD,
　　because he has dealt bountifully with me.

　　　　　　　　　　　　　　　　　(Ps 13:1–2, 5–6)

Similar to the words of the psalmist is the following prayer from Mother Teresa of Calcutta:

Lord, my God, who am I that You should forsake me? The Child of Love—and now become as the most hated one—the one—You have thrown away as unwanted—unloved. I call, I cling, I want—and there is no One to answer—no One on Whom I can cling.... Where is my Faith—even deep down right in there is nothing, but emptiness & darkness...?*

---

*Mother Teresa, *Mother Teresa: Come Be My Light: The Private Writings of the Saint of Calcutta* (New York: Image, 2009), 187.

Have you ever prayed this kind of prayer or experienced a time when you thought God was totally absent from your life? Mother Teresa wrote this prayer in her journal after her confessor suggested she write a prayer to Jesus. Doubters and believers alike can draw something from her prayer. This same type of experience Mother Teresa described happens in the lives of many people who are so dedicated and devoted.

While Mother Teresa had this dark side to her, this feeling of such emptiness, she herself tried to understand this absence, and concluded that God allowed her to go through this experience because the people to whom she was ministering felt the absence of God. She wondered how she could ever identify with them—how she could ever have any sense of solidarity with them—if she herself did not feel the painful agony of the absence of God.

It is not surprising that atheists and agnostics see the darkness of Mother Teresa's life as proof that God does not exist. Believers, however, can find encouragement in Mother Teresa's torment. It is also interesting to note that the absence of Christ's voice in her life never swayed her from her mission, to which she remained committed until her death. In fact, her perseverance may be as important in the ministry she rendered to this world as was her ministry to the poor of Calcutta.

If we are honest with ourselves and honest with each other, *every person* has his or her cross to bear as a part of the journey in life. As we strive to live the Christian life and engage ourselves on this pilgrimage of following God, we will have experiences like this—suffering from emotional and physical paralysis as we long for God.

In one of his sermons, my priest friend Papayiorgi (Father George) offered an analogy of how we grow spiritually. In essence, he said, "God gives form and shape to our faith in the same way a blacksmith does when he puts a piece of iron in the fire. The blacksmith hammers, molds, and shapes the iron into a much stronger piece of steel." The truth is that these kinds of experiences temper us and make us stronger. We must, however, not panic and run away from the experience. We pray for God's will to be done and wait for his answer.

Does this waiting mean that we do nothing? No. We do wait on some occasions, but while we wait, we must be active. We must seek the Lord when we wait actively. Mother Teresa is a perfect example of someone who worked faithfully at the task given to her by God, even when she felt his absence.

The psalms often speak about seeking the face of God. Does God play hide-and-seek with us? Does God deliberately hide himself and play games with us, making it hard to find him?

Let's take a look at just a few from Psalm 14, a corollary to Psalm 13:

> Fools say in their hearts, "There is no God."…
> The LORD looks down from heaven on humankind
>   to see if there are any who are wise,
>   who seek after God.
>
> (vv. 1–2)

Here, the "fool" is not just a few isolated people. In reality, the fool is all of us. There are times we all act as if God does not exist. When we treat God as if he were absent, he will certainly seem absent. Nevertheless, God does invite us and wants us to be a part of his plan. God wants to find us. He *will* find us and never stops seeking.

FOR CONSIDERATION

1. On cloudy days when the sun is not visible, does it mean that the sun is gone? No. We must believe in the presence of the sun even when we cannot see it. Likewise, we must believe in the presence of God even when we cannot feel his nearness. Experiencing the absence of God gives us an opportunity to grow in our faith. That was certainly the case with the disciples.

2. To experience the presence of God, we pray. As we wait for our prayers to be answered, we must continue to pray. Have you felt as though your prayers were not getting through to God at all? Most of us have had a similar experience.

3. When you experience this, feeling emotional or physical pain, feeling rejected or abandoned—when we question God's presence or absence—seek comfort from people who have had a similar experience.

4. The story of Zacchaeus that we read in Luke 19 tells us of the human need to seek God and God's desire to seek and save his people. Because he was short, Zacchaeus climbed a tree to see Jesus. Jesus saw him and asked him to come down from the tree and said, "Zacchaeus, hurry and come down; for I must stay at your house today" (v. 5). Zacchaeus repented and restored his life, and Jesus said, "Today salvation has come to this house" (v. 9). Not only are we seeking God, but God is also seeking us.

CHAPTER 12

In Times of Crisis

NOTHING SAPS OUR energy like a crisis, which can drain us and make us feel as if we simply can't go on. A crisis can take many forms, but essentially it is a problem or a situation presenting difficulty or uncertainty that needs a solution. For example, some years ago, I remember consulting a professional when one of my sons was failing in school, causing a problem in our family life. Hearing my concern that my son was determined to drop out of school, Dr. Herbert Holt looked at me with a smile and said, "You and I left our parents behind in their homeland, and we came to America to make a life of our own. And we did what we wanted. I suggest that you give your son five hundred dollars and tell him to go west and come back rich." I pondered Dr. Holt's advice, and what I thought he meant was to let my son do what he wanted and suffer the consequences.

It took me a long time to understand and accept Dr. Holt's wisdom that we should not try to push our children into our mold of success, but rather let them experience life on their own terms. We cannot make them into small versions of ourselves or into the people we wish we had been. God gives us freedom to be authentically ourselves. We must give our children the same freedom.

As a father, I advised my son not to quit school, because of the opportunities of having an education. I also advised that since a bad choice can take two years to correct, to avoid making bad choices. Eventually, I had to let my son go and design his own life the way he chose.

Facing the reality of a problem often provides options for how we can find a viable solution and regain peace. In some cases, a crisis in life can be more serious and present a problem or emergency requiring immediate remedial action. For example, two years ago, my wife, Pat, was diagnosed with cancer in the pelvic bone. She was treated effectively with chemotherapy, and eventually her doctor informed her that the cancer was in remission. Both of us were very happy, and we celebrated joyfully the event of her recovery, which coincided with our birthdays and our thirty-sixth wedding anniversary. Truly these happy events brought great joy to us and to our family.

About three weeks later, a biopsy indicated that the lymphoma had returned. Fortunately, the lymphoma was still confined only to her pelvic bone as originally found. With an already weak immune system, the new plan was a combination of three or four sessions of chemotherapy at Memorial Sloan Kettering in New York City, spaced three weeks apart. Following that would be a biopsy to determine that the tumors were totally gone, and then a bone marrow transplant, which would involve five weeks of hospital isolation. The great news was that this procedure was not new, and it has been quite successful for others, something that gave my wife greater hope for recovery.

Besides the dedicated doctors and the excellent hospital personnel, Pat's treatment was accompanied by the fervent prayers of many loving people. Pat and I felt God's presence, as family and several of our dear friends had gracefully volunteered to help and be available for any possible emergency.

Within two weeks, Pat felt better and was sent to Hope Lodge, a wonderful facility in New York City for patients recovering from cancer. Following this, it will take at least six months, perhaps as long as two years, to rebuild a new immune system. While we are still in critical times, we pray to our Lord Jesus to extend his healing arm and embrace Pat during her treatments, strengthening and restoring her health.

Believing that God is in charge, we derive a great deal of comfort as we pray and read verses from the Bible. God promises to give us the strength we need to get through trying times. The psalmist echoes this truth that God is our source of power for facing any battle in life: "The LORD is my light and my salvation; / whom shall I fear? / The LORD is the stronghold of my life; / of whom shall I be afraid?" (Ps 27:1).

St. Paul reminds us, "I can do all things through him who strengthens me" (Phil 4:13), and James writes, "My brothers and sisters, whenever you face trials of any kind, consider it nothing but joy" (Jas 1:2), because trials produce faith and develop perseverance, and our sense of God's presence increases, as does our joy in it. By taking the word of God into our being—consistently internalizing God's word and applying it in our life—we become aware that there are no other resolutions.

In view of our human condition, whenever a crisis occurs—especially a serious problem where we have little control—we can respond by reflecting on the scriptures and asking God, first, to give us the strength we need to assess properly and endure the crisis; and, second, to draw us closer to him, the source of healing. Faith in God's love and mercy helps to rise above any possible crisis.

Cancer is the word nobody likes to hear. From a technical standpoint, cancer is a change in the normal growth of cells, causing them to spread and destroy healthy tissues and organs. But from an emotional perspective, cancer is one of the most devastating experiences a person and his or her family may have to endure. It is not exactly a death sentence, which is the first thing many people think when a medical professional gives them the serious news. Thanks to advances in research and development, many types of cancer that were virtually incurable several years ago are now treatable—if caught early enough. So there is reason for hope. Still, cancer can be devastating to the individual and the family. If you or a member of your family or a close friend has suffered from cancer, you understand the emotional and even physical impact of this illness.

Pat and I learned a lot about ourselves when the news about the second appearance of cancer occurred. Our faith that God cares about the suffering of his people was of great comfort. We believe that God will not abandon Pat. God marvelously and miraculously cares for her as he does for each and every one of us. In such times of crisis, the words of the Prophet Isaiah are comforting: "Can a woman forget her nursing child, / or show no compassion for the child of her womb? / Even these may forget, / yet I will not forget you. / See, I have inscribed you on the palms of my hands; / your walls are continually before me. / Your builders outdo your destroyers, / and those who laid you waste go away from you" (Isa 49:15–17). God says to us and to my dear wife, Pat, "I love you. You are precious in your fragility and in your current critical condition. Your being is a gift. I breathe into you and hold you as something precious. Be at peace."

Although on the surface, we tried to appear brave, we experienced another set of feelings: a fear of the dreaded disease and having to come face-to-face with life and death. Over the years, we have watched several members of our community, some relatives, and other close friends battle cancer. Although each one had a different form of the disease, they shared much in common—primarily the fact that all were people of faith. It did not matter whether they had a strong or a mediocre faith in God when they received their first diagnosis. As their treatment—and in some cases, the disease—progressed, so did their faith and trust in God's healing presence. Though they suffered from the physical effects of the disease and the potency of the treatment, the nonphysical part of their selves, their spiritual self, gained strength. The true meaning of St. Paul's statement became evident: "So we do not lose heart. Even though our outer nature is wasting away, our inner nature is being renewed day by day. For this slight momentary affliction is preparing us for an eternal weight of glory beyond all measure" (2 Cor 4:16–17).

Regardless of the outcome, each of our family members and friends gave us a glimpse of God's presence in our life. God reached out to us through our relatives and friends, who helped and comforted us. With gratitude, we thank God for his mercy and continue to pray for Pat's total recovery.

FOR CONSIDERATION

1. Let's face the truth: fear is our root problem in the midst of any crisis. Why do we fear? The enormity and frequency of difficulties and challenges in our lives are part of life itself and should be faced with less fear, for God is in charge. The choice to trust God in the midst of our crises is ours.

2. As Christians, we need a spiritual response to the stress responses that result from crises in our lives. We need to experience God's perspective, spiritual strength, and wisdom in daily living to prepare us for critical times. Pray regularly, meditate on the scriptures, and learn from the heroes of faith in early church history.

3. Relying on God has to begin again every day as if we had never done it. We need to trust that Jesus is there for us in times of crisis. "Remember, I am with you always, to the end of the age" (Matt 28:20). This reminder from Christ is reassuring and can prepare us to respond when crisis and fear come into our lives.

4. God offers us peace in the midst of tragedy or sorrow. "Peace I leave with you; my peace I give to you. I do not give to you as the world gives. Do not let your hearts be troubled, and do not let them be afraid" (John 14:27). We need to ask for his peace, not the peace that the world promises. A crisis can be a new beginning.

5. Here is a prayer that I find helpful in times of crises:

O heavenly King, O Comforter, the Spirit of truth,
you who are present in all places and fill all things;
Treasury of good things and Giver of life:
Come and dwell in us and cleanse us from every stain,
visit and heal our infirmities,
save our souls and make our bodies well,
and deliver us from tribulation, evil, and distress,
O gracious Lord. Amen.*

---

*"Invocation of the Holy Spirit." Every service of the Orthodox Church, with the exception of the seven sacraments, starts with the Invocation of the Holy Spirit.

CHAPTER 13

The Power of Prayer

Prayer promotes a relationship with God and provides for us true knowledge of God. It is the connecting link between the human and the divine. The strength of prayer lies in the intention of our heart. Prayer can be a petition to God for something we need and believe is good for us to have. God does not need to be reminded of our needs. He knows our needs before we ask him.

"Prayer is the light of the soul," claims St. John Chrysostom, a church father of the fourth century. His eloquence echoes through the ages, reaching our ears today and warming our hearts. "There is nothing more worthwhile than to pray to God and to converse with him, for prayer unites us with God."* Prayer is the unique channel of communication through which we become more conscious of God. Through prayer, we learn of God's great love for us, and we find comfort, peace, and joy in his presence. From age to age in every land and culture, human beings reach out through various means to connect with their Creator. Something in the human heart yearns to understand the origins of the universe, the beginning and the purpose of life.

In our high-tech times, as we employ the latest electronic devices to communicate with the world around us—and we do

---

*St. John Chrysostom, Homily 6 on Prayer, "Prayer Is the Light of the Soul," http://www.vatican.va/spirit/documents/spirit_20010302_giovanni-crisostomo_en.html.

this remarkably well—the spirit within us emerges and yearns for what is more, for what is good, beautiful, real, and lasting. As noted earlier, made as we are in the image and likeness of God, "Our hearts are restless, until they can find rest in [God]," claims St. Augustine. Prayer is a human journey back to God. It is a personal journey we take in time among our fellow travelers, but it is also a timeless journey we take alone toward eternity. Through prayer, we discern the truth of our own spiritual identity, the inseparable relationship of God and his people. Through prayer, we connect with the ultimate reality, God, and discover who we are in his creation, giving us a sense of belonging—we are his people, and he is our Father. He gives us life, heals the sick and afflicted, and reforms the sinner. Our Lord Jesus Christ urges us to watch and pray—that is, always to be alert and keep in touch with God, the Source of life. He emphasizes the need for persistence in prayer. "Ask, and it will be given you; search, and you will find; knock, and the door will be opened for you. For everyone who asks receives, and everyone who searches finds, and for everyone who knocks, the door will be opened" (Matt 7:7–8).

When we pray for things that are good and beneficial to our spiritual life, our prayers are answered. God knows the difference between wants and needs far better than we do. What we truly need, we will have, and prayer based on spiritual understanding helps us become more conscious of the good that is already ours and at hand.

True prayer promotes inner harmony. When we free ourselves from materialistic needs, we become more aware of our spiritual identity. Then we know that we are praying correctly and effectively. If, on the other hand, wants and human desires still seem to elude us, we should not give up. A deeper understanding of our true being as a spiritual entity is on the way! In the meantime, we must know that God loves us and is taking care of us. Through genuine prayer, we strengthen our faith in

God's goodness and his wish for us to have joy and peace. As we pray, Christ becomes our companion in everyday life, protecting, enlightening, and strengthening us. It is an intimate journey.

As his people, we must pray personally and privately, or as Christ has taught us, in secret. As we pray alone, behind closed doors—not merely in our rooms but in the room of our hearts—we experience that special intimacy. Then our dialogue becomes real. We reveal our innermost secrets, requests, needs, and problems. We ask God for anything. Nothing is too small or insignificant. But we must ask with faith, convinced that God does hear our prayers and answers in the way known only to him. Sometimes we are impatient and want God to answer our requests immediately; that's human nature. Like children, we demand things. But God has his own plans for us and takes his time to respond. If our prayers go unanswered, it does not mean that God is ignoring our requests. God's delay is not denial. God may not answer prayers that could prove destructive. As C. S. Lewis, a prolific Christian writer, once wrote, "Prayer is request. The essence of request, as distinct from compulsion, is that it may or may not be granted." Furthermore, he continues, "Invariable 'success' in prayer…would prove something much more like magic—a power in human beings to control, or compel, the course of nature."*

When we ask God to give us what we need and to enable us to fulfill his will, we cease placing demands on him. God reveals his will to our minds. He opens the way for us to follow. He removes the obstacles. As we acknowledge our faults and shortcomings, we experience the satisfaction of his forgiveness. He is a God of love, compassion, and mercy.

Once we turn toward God in prayer, the joy of his love will begin to blossom in our heart. Our Lord Jesus Christ, God in

---

*C. S. Lewis, "The World's Last Night," in *The Essential C. S. Lewis*, ed. Lyle W. Dorsett (New York: Scribner, 1996), 379.

human nature, modeled for us the idea of prayer. He prayed regularly. In the Sermon on the Mount, we read Christ's primary teaching pertinent to prayer:

> And whenever you pray, do not be like the hypocrites; for they love to stand and pray in the synagogues and at the street corners, so that they may be seen by others. Truly I tell you, they have received their reward. But whenever you pray, go into your room and shut the door and pray to your Father who is in secret; and your Father who sees in secret will reward you.
>
> When you are praying, do not heap up empty phrases as the Gentiles do; for they think that they will be heard because of their many words. Do not be like them, for your Father knows what you need before you ask him. (Matt 6:5–8)

Since childhood we have learned that we must pray, yet we sometimes are uncertain as to how to pray. Simply, it is good to be brief in our prayer. Brevity brings humility while ensuring that we accomplish that which we are really capable of accomplishing. It can also prevent us from falling into despair over asking for too much. The length of our prayers is not significant, but rather the spirit in which they are offered.

It is also good to be regular in our prayer, setting aside a certain time for prayer each day, and thereby ensuring continuity in our awareness and presence before God. Regular prayer serves to remind us that we belong to God, and without his presence our life is empty and without direction. Prayer acquaints us with Christ. Like the Apostle Paul, as we pray, we become intimately acquainted with Christ: "I want to know Christ and the power of his resurrection and the sharing of his sufferings by becoming like him in his death" (Phil 3:10).

Through prayer, we become intimately involved with Christ. Our soul yearns for a relationship with Christ that only constant prayer can achieve.

> Trust in the LORD with all your heart,
>   and do not rely on your own insight.
> In all your ways acknowledge him,
>   and he will make straight your paths.
>
> (Prov 3:5–6)

FOR CONSIDERATION

1. To start a life of prayer, learn to exercise the discipline of simplicity. Be spontaneous and use your own words to connect with God.

2. You don't have to use a dictionary to discover fancy words. Your simple vocabulary suffices. Let your heart do the talking.

3. Seek solitude. Find a quiet place and use it for your private prayer. You need no environmental distractions. A Bible, a cross, or an icon of Christ may inspire your thoughts for prayer.

4. Focus your thoughts on what you would like to pray about, and start your prayer. Take a couple of deep breaths before you start and relax in God's presence.

5. When you say the Lord's Prayer and you get to "Thy will be done," pause for a second and say,

> Lord, in every hour of the day
> reveal Your will to me.
> Teach me to treat all that comes to me throughout the day
> with peace of soul.
> Guide my thoughts and feelings
> and let me not forget
> that You are in charge. Amen.

ACTION

"The bread which you do not use is the bread of the hungry; the garment hanging in your wardrobe is the garment of him who is naked; the shoes that you do not wear are the shoes of the one who is barefoot; the money that you keep locked away is the money of the poor; the acts of charity that you do not perform are so many injustices that you commit."

—Saint Basil the Great

CHAPTER 14

Grace

DURING A BITTERLY cold winter one year, I recall that stress sapped my whole being as the weather forecasters predicted that we would be getting eight inches of snow. My wife tested the snow blower, and it was working well, ready for action. That was some comfort. Meanwhile, I tried to get my car started so that I could go to work, but the car door would not open. It was frozen and, as I tried to open it, my fingers were freezing. Suddenly the sun emerged from the clouds, and I felt the warmth on my back. I stepped aside to let the sun hit the car door. A few minutes later, the unexpected happened; the door opened, and when I got into the car, I felt warmer. I paused for a few seconds and thanked God for his blessing.

A familiar thought surfaced: *each day of our life begins with God's grace.* God's grace is much like the sun. It is always with us, but we are not always aware of its presence. In difficult times, when we are stressed by heavy schedules and unfinished tasks or when we are undergoing a mental or physical crisis, we can be easily distracted, and uncertainty or pain clouds our vision. Somehow, we can miss God's grace in our good times as well as in our bad times. But God is always present in our lives. He does not wait for our heads to clear or our problems to be solved. His grace, like our breath, keeps us alive, up and around, embracing us, directing us, and strengthening us to meet our daily needs.

Grace can appear unexpectedly in a phone call or a letter from a friend, in a warm hug from a loved one, or in a comforting word at the right time. In small and different ways, we need to be reminded how much God loves and provides for us. But we need to be vigilant and always look for God's gift of grace.

The true meaning of grace derives from the Greek, *charis*. In modern Greek, *charis* comes from the verb *chairo*, which means "to rejoice." Gradually it came to signify "favor," "goodwill," and "loving kindness"—especially as granted by a superior to an inferior.

In the New Testament, the word *grace* appears 156 times, and it takes on a special redemptive sense in which God makes his love available to all humanity while his power sustains the universe. There is tremendous emphasis on the fact that human happiness is the result of divine grace, a wonderful truth that should never be minimized. At the same time, it must not be distorted. We often hear, "By the grace of God" I'm still here, or I have accomplished this or that or something important. For Paul, grace is that expression of the divine love that appears in the coming of Christ to deal with human sin and estrangement. His grace was and still is for everyone, according to each individual's needs.

Grace is hard to define, for it really needs to be understood at a personal level. In essence, grace is the truth that God unconditionally accepts and loves us. Divine grace, the work of the Holy Spirit, is God's gift to everyone who is willing to receive it for his or her own wellness and ultimate salvation. Our response to grace is our acts of love, which are the fruits of the Holy Spirit. By divine grace, we understand the saving and deifying energy of God made available through Christ's mission and distributed by the Holy Spirit, who continues to be our source of grace and sanctification.

God's grace has been offered to the entire human family. St. Paul says, "God, who had set me apart before I was born and called me through his grace, was pleased to reveal his Son to me, so that I might proclaim him among the Gentiles" (Gal 1:15–16). For Paul, God's grace meant forgiveness for his former life, unconditional acceptance and love for him, and dynamic motivation to go into a pagan world and preach the gospel. Later, he writes to his disciple Titus, "For the grace of God has appeared, bringing salvation to all" (Titus 2:11). What this suggests is that God's grace is potentially available to all who care to access it (see Rom 5:1; 6:3–4, 17). Paul affirmed that grace is accessed by faith (see Rom 5:1–2; Eph 2:8–9). It is not, however, a faith void of a loving response to God; it is a faith that acts out of love (see Jas 2:21–26). God's grace is not dispensed apart from an instruction that requires understanding and obedience. While God extends grace, human beings must be willing to "receive" the favor (2 Cor 6:1), claims St. Paul. When this concept is truly grasped, service to God will flow with a freshness and zeal that invigorate the soul. Doubtless, a failure to fathom the true significance of grace is the reason that many believers are spiritually lethargic.

Salvation is indeed the most extraordinary expression of God's grace. Salvation is of divine origin, but it is not anything that God was bound to arrange by the necessity of his nature. It is the result of his gracious will. Had it not been for his grace, salvation would never have come. "For by grace you have been saved through faith, and this is not your own doing; it is the gift of God" (Eph 2:8). The Greek grammar denotes not the act of being saved but the fact of having been saved. God's grace rather than human merit is the source of the whole arrangement. Salvation is a gift; it is not earned. Grace is the free and unmerited favor of God as manifested in the salvation of sinners and the bestowing of blessings. It is God's gift granted to sinners for their salvation. Common Christian teaching is that grace is unmerited mercy (favor) that God gave to humanity by sending his Son to die on a cross, thus delivering eternal salvation.

What is truly meant by the grace of God? When we speak of God's grace, we mean all the good gifts that we enjoy freely in life. There are so many that we could spend a lifetime celebrating them. A better approach is to affirm that life itself, with all its delights, is the fundamental gift. For us, the gift of life includes the wondrous gift of being human, finding ourselves in the midst of the larger gift of creation. That is the bedrock of grace—creation of the world, life, human beings. As humans, we are given a unique place in the created order. The creation stories in Genesis are ways of celebrating this original grace. In these stories, God pronounces all creation, including humankind, very good—that is, full of grace.

We also use the word *grace* to mean the secondary gifts we perceive in the skill and intelligence of creatures. When we speak of the beauty of a lion, a tiger, or any animal or creature, we say that they exude a grace, discerned in the vitality and fluidity of their existence and movement. When we use the word *graceful* to describe a creature, it's because the creature is being expressive of its God-given self.

Another way of speaking about grace is more about redemption than about creation. Whereas God pronounced original grace, the other side of the story is when we head off on our own, ignoring the Giver. We call this headstrong straying *original sin*, meaning our freedom to choose the not so good, to turn aside from original grace. Ironically, this freedom is itself the most unique grace given to humankind by God, the capacity to choose our own way, which must necessarily entail the possibility of choosing poorly. Because we have not always chosen the most graceful path, we have ended up in some miserable blind alleys along the way. When we grasp our predicament and call for the help we had previously spurned, amazing grace comes to our rescue.

FOR CONSIDERATION

1. Every virtue, including that imitation of Christ that is within our power, prepares us for divine union. It is still grace that tends to accomplish the unutterable union itself. By means of grace, all of God co-dwells within all those who are worthy.

2. Believers may receive God in his totality, and as a kind of reward for their struggles in ascending to him, they possess him, himself alone, who has made them worthy of becoming his members, and he dwells within them.

3. We are saved by grace. As members of the human family, we were justly condemned to death for sin and disobedience. However, salvation comes through faith in God's revealed purpose in his Son, who died for all. Nothing apart from faith would enable our receiving of the gift of salvation.

4. Grace is the empowering presence of God, enabling us to be who he created us to be, and to do what he has called us to do. Alternatively, grace gives us the desire and the power that God gives us to do his will for our personal benefit.

5. Our Lord Jesus Christ is Savior, Redeemer, and Sanctifier. He is not putting on different masks or costumes or personae to play different roles. Jesus Christ, God in human form, expresses the totality of God's own Being and character in grace.

CHAPTER 15

Surviving Suffering

AS MY WIFE'S COMPANION and caregiver, visiting both the hospital and Hope Lodge frequently was often a very daunting experience. The agony and the anticipated anxiety were evident and varied in each person's eyes. With each of my visits to the hospital and Hope Lodge, I became increasingly aware and mindful of the suffering that permeates our world in addition to cancer.

Suffering is a fact of life—a multifaceted affliction that has affected humanity since the beginning of time. Suffering on earth is a uniquely human experience. Only human beings suffer. Animals have pain, but they do not suffer emotionally in the way we might think. By instinct, they seek comfort in their own species or in nature.

Our world will always have suffering. We tend to look on suffering as something to be avoided at all costs. Surely we need to make an effort to remove suffering whenever and wherever we can in our lives and those of others. Yet if we could by some miracle remove suffering from our world, there would still remain pain in childbirth, torments in illness, and anguish in death. Sadness, longing, and heartache would not disappear. They would be lessened greatly but never ended. This result should not discourage us but rather cause us to see suffering—and our role in decreasing it—differently. Through the eyes of faith in a loving God, we are able to see suffering's larger purpose, whereby it is transformed and transmuted, becoming redemptive and bringing comfort. We often grow through the experience of suffering: emotionally, mentally, spiritually, and morally—that is, when we let the suffering ennoble us rather than embitter us.

Trying to define suffering is like trying to define love, faith, hope—even God. In fact, suffering is much too deep and mysterious to be contained in a mere definition. In a personal, limited way, we can tell what suffering is as it occurs in each individual.

Our life brings moments of some unavoidable physical sufferings, beginning with birth itself: from the moment we emerge from the womb, we suffer physical pain, and only God knows what emotional stress we endure as infants. A baby cries to communicate hunger and his or her needs. As children, we may get dropped or burned, or feel rejected and abandoned by parents or another caregiver. Teenagers may feel utterly frustrated and dejected if their parents won't let them attend a late-night party, watch certain movies, or buy a certain style of clothes. Nobody survives the teenage years without some emotional scars. The damage may be permanent, but it is not fatal. As adults, we go through periods of confusion: *Will I find someone to love me? Will the person to whom I feel attracted and wish to marry be the right mate? Will I be happy? Will I find the right job? What will my future be like?* We also feel unhappy when we cannot pay our bills, frustrated when our job bores us, or lonely when our relationships are unfulfilling or complicated. All these experiences are examples of mental suffering—summed up as painful feelings that arise from being separated from the people we love, having to be with people we don't like, or not getting what we want. Feelings of insecurity lead to anxiety, concern, and sometimes depression.

Satisfaction and happiness tend to characterize one's youth and senior years, but the middle years often leave us in a trough. We may go through a life crisis—something that disrupts our personal, mental, and emotional health, alters the course of our lives, and affects us for a long time. During this period, intimate relationships can break, families can become dysfunctional, and marriages can come to an end.

Many people resort to therapy in midlife, seeking comfort and direction. As they establish a therapeutic alliance with a seasoned therapist, their lifestyle changes. Although many professionals have defined midlife crisis as a theoretical construct, for many people the experience is quite real. The significance of midlife is that adults are coming to realize their own mortality. Many people realize they have reached a midpoint in their life-span and experience internal conflicts or dissatisfaction because of unrealized goals, negative self-perceptions, or physical limitations as a result of aging or health issues. The crisis is unique because it largely relates to an age group. Yet certain wisdom surfaces from such a crisis, and when we let wisdom meet the grace of God, love and freedom become possible.

The fear of death or the death of a loved one, the decline in physical strength and vitality, dissatisfaction at work, or the shortage of available jobs are more likely to affect people in this age group and present a critical life dilemma. For some people, the effects of crises prove to be beneficial. These people courageously move forward and find new jobs, and their quality of life improves. Others experience more negative effects. They lose courage, see the glass as half empty, and become emotionally paralyzed or depressed. When people experience a midlife crisis, a positive approach may prove beneficial to reassess their achievements in terms of their dreams. The result may be a desire to make significant changes in areas such as career, work-life balance, marriage, romantic relationships, finances, or physical appearance.

So, what is suffering? When we approach suffering with humility, we have an opportunity for wisdom. As I become aware of my own vulnerability and inability to define or find meaning in times of physical or emotional suffering, I reflect on the life of Jesus, whose earthly life translates God's love in action—serving other people, preaching, teaching, healing, and performing miracles. By the third year of his ministry, he is enveloped in a storm, about which he had foretold to his disciples. He was arrested, flogged, mocked, crowned with thorns, and nailed to the cross. Jesus did not control any or part of his passion. His suffering ended in the crucifixion and was followed by his glorious resurrection. Our suffering, any kind of storm we go through, will end and will offer us a new and meaningful life.

In contemplating the life of Jesus, I am reminded of the following story:

> On that day, when evening had come, he said to them, "Let us go across to the other side." And leaving the crowd behind, they took him with them in the boat, just as he was. Other boats were with him. A great windstorm arose, and the waves beat into the boat, so that the boat was already being swamped. But he was in the stern, asleep on the cushion; and they woke him up and said to him, "Teacher, do you not care that we are perishing?" He woke up and rebuked the wind, and said to the sea, "Peace! Be still!" Then the wind ceased, and there was a dead calm. He said to them, "Why are you afraid? Have you still no faith?" And they were filled with great awe and said to one another, "Who then is this, that even the wind and the sea obey him." (Mark 4:35–41)

In sharing this passage with my wife, we both found comfort and hope, and were reminded that it is unrealistic to think that we can avoid the storms of life. Furthermore, noticing the disciples' reaction to the storm—their fear that they could possibly drown—

offered us another lesson. Fear is such a human feeling when confronted by a stormy event in our life. Like the disciples, we forget that Jesus Christ is our ever constant companion. He said to them, "Let's go across to the other side." The "other side" for all of us could mean the side of a healthier and more peaceful life. Jesus, fully aware that the storm was imminent, could have spared the disciples a great deal of distress and anguish if he had said, "Look, there's a really big storm coming, so let's remain on land until it passes." Rather, he deliberately led the disciples through that storm, leaving us with a lesson that he is our companion during our lifetime, in which there will be trials and tribulations.

Another important consideration is that their destination was not the storm itself, but rather the other side of the lake. Some pain and suffering are inevitable in our earthly journey. Do not lose courage, and let your heart hear his words: "I am with you always, to the end of the age" (Matt 28:20).

FOR CONSIDERATION

1. We may like to believe that we are entitled to a life of comfort—that a life consisting of suffering is simply unfair. Who likes an unfair world? If we believe that life is about growth and growth entails a degree of pain, then nothing is unfair about it.

2. Suffering has a therapeutic aspect. As we go through it, we discover that we are not alone in this world. We have people who care, and our own well-being cannot be our main purpose in

life. Well-being in a vacuum, separated from interpersonal relationships, is nothing.

3. No suffering can defeat us if we are prepared to search for its meaning. No loss is conceivable that does not hold the possibility of at least one meaning; God has a plan for each member of his creation. He is in charge of our life, and will never let us down. In spite of life's adversities, be grateful for what you have, and trust in God's presence in your life.

4. People undergoing physical or emotional suffering seek from strangers what they can no longer find in a firm faith or from people close to them. However, where scientific knowledge fails, an empathic and loving God is the answer.

5. Finally, based especially on faith, there is spiritual suffering to which the great mystics were the best and most eloquent witnesses. Here, suffering is in the innermost part of one's being. Suffering is the part of life that makes us more fully human.

CHAPTER 16

Touched by God

ALTHOUGH GOD COULD instantly give us feelings of his presence, in the long run, it wouldn't help. Our faith must be the bedrock of the word of God, not the shifting sands of feelings. Emotions tend to fluctuate. God's word is solid, and the only way anyone can be a solid believer is to place feelings in perspective and hold onto God's word. If you want to feel moved and experience God's presence, a good start is to reflect on the scriptures.

The Gospels offer strong evidence of people who experienced the presence of God. Jairus, for example, was a synagogue official whose daughter was dying, and was willing and ready to do anything to save her life. The doctors did not understand her illness. He hastened to Jesus, dropped to his knees, and pleaded earnestly, "My little daughter is at the point of death. Come and lay your hands on her, so that she may be made well, and live" (Mark 5:23). Meanwhile, his daughter died, but Jesus, aware of this father's faith, came to his home and raised her from the dead.

Another example is the woman afflicted with hemorrhages for twelve years and had visited all the doctors possible. She spent all her money without being healed. She had heard about Jesus and believed in him and began to think, "If I but touch his clothes, I will be made well" (Mark 5:28). She found herself in the presence of Jesus; she walked up to him, touched his cloak (a gesture of strong faith), and felt well. Jesus turned around and demanded to know who touched him. The disciples intervened, saying, many people have touched you. But Jesus was aware that power had gone forth from him. The woman in fear and trembling told Jesus the whole truth. Jesus said to her, "Daughter, your faith has made you well; go in peace, and be healed of your disease" (Mark 5:34). The change that she felt within herself was her healing.

After the crucifixion, sad and disappointed that Jesus, their teacher, had suffered a terrible death, Luke and Cleopas, two of Jesus' followers, were on their way to Emmaus. They were walking along the road that led about seven miles from Jerusalem. A stranger drew near and walked with them. They were visibly sad, and the stranger empathized with their grief. They felt themselves moved by the healing words of this man who was so well versed in the scriptures. Being that it was late, they invited him to spend the evening with them. Jesus accepted the invitation. They did not recognize him until the moment when he was at table with them. He took bread in his hands, blessed and broke it, and gave it to them. Then their eyes were opened and they recognized him, and he vanished from their sight. They said to each other, "Were not our hearts burning within us while he was talking to us on the road, while he was opening the scriptures to us?" (Luke 24:32).

The voice of Jesus is essential on the spiritual journey. Jesus left a model that we can imitate. I am the way: *I am the path that you should follow that you may have complete joy within you*; I am the truth: *listen and obey my teaching*, and I am the life: *I came to give you real and everlasting life* (see John 14:6). We cannot be Jesus Christ, but we can imitate his virtues of caring, kindness, compassion, forgiveness, and love.

Jesus showed us how to live, how to be, and how to love. With divine authority he said, "This is my commandment, that you love one another as I have loved you. No one has greater love than this, to lay down one's life for one's friends. You are my friends if you do what I command you" (John 15:12–14).

As we noted earlier, God made us in his own image. He has made us his cocreators. We can thus find within ourselves the riches that exist in God, and if we can find them in ourselves, we can also find them in others, whether they are aware that they possess these riches or not. God is so present in us, so identified with our lives, that if he were to withdraw, life would be annihilated. God is not only the principle of life but also the principle of its conservation, its duration, and its progress.

God's providence watches over each one of us. This goodness does not depend on our degree of understanding nor on our collaboration. Whether we practice our faith or not; whether we are atheists or unbelievers; whether we are indifferent, oblivious, tepid, slothful and treacherous, or fervent and committed to his service, we will enjoy the same benefits, the same temperature, and the same gardens, and have the right to the same measuring stick. Our efforts will be rewarded according to the use we make of our intelligence and will. The sun shines on everyone; rain falls on all doorsteps; cold penetrates all walls; heat affects every person because all of us, without exception, are made in the image and likeness of God.

I have known Father Michael for more than thirty-five years. He is a graduate of Princeton Theological School with a doctoral degree in theology, a well-respected priest and pastor in one of the largest cathedrals in the United States. When he called and asked to come to my office for therapy, I felt both curious and honored.

In reflecting on his prayer and the feeling of God's presence, he said, "Sometimes I feel like God just isn't there."

"I wonder how you must feel," I said, "if you find yourself discouraged at times, because it seems like God just isn't around."

"When I deal with drama, often seeing people of different ages who suffer mentally and physically, I ask, 'God, where are you? Why do you allow so much pain?'" Father Michael shook his head with evident sadness in his face. He cleared his throat and said, "Recently, I saw a young woman who suffered from severe depression. She went from one doctor to another looking for relief. One doctor gave her antidepressant medicine. When she felt a little better, she came to see me a couple of times, and each time, she asked me to pray for her and I did. But my prayers had no effect. Two days later, she overdosed and died in her sleep. I feel that her tormented soul probably wanted to liberate itself and escape her body. When I performed her funeral, I felt her parents' ultimate pain."

"It seems that you absorbed some of their pain," I said.

"I have sleepless nights. My prayers for those people don't seem to help," he said in utter disappointment.

"Do unanswered prayers cause you to think that God has checked out of your life?" I asked.

"I have a hard time believing that a loving God who claims that he will never leave us or forsake us [Heb 13:5] can be so far away from human suffering," he said. "Early this morning, a mother came to our rectory crying and asking for help. She is a single parent with a daughter, sixteen, who got pregnant with a fifteen-year-old boy who she was helping in math. 'Father, what shall I do? She is still too young to be a mother. Please tell me what to do.' I hesitated to offer an answer, for my mind kept thinking that it is God's design....Then I had another disturbing thought: *I wish God would do much more besides giving life, and intervene to stop all sorts of innocent people from making bad choices and suffering.*"

"I'm truly sad to hear that you don't feel God's presence," I said with a sense of empathy. "If you think you're the only one to feel that way, please don't. I certainly have felt isolation and separation from God. Sometimes it was the result of my guilty conscience. Other times, I felt that calamity had unfairly fallen on me and wondered if God really loved or cared about my situation."

Father Michael smiled, and I realized that he felt comforted being in the presence of another person, a therapist, who had a similar struggle. Sensing that the ground appeared fertile to plant some seeds of relief, I decided to share a personal example of God's caring love—God's presence—to give him a human example that I hoped would be positive and supportive. At the risk of giving God human attitudes, making him in our image and likeness, I shared the story of being a parent as I recall it many years ago. "My wife and I were blessed with a daughter. We both loved her dearly and cherished her early years of growing. When she became a teenager, we became seriously protective, and during her sixteenth and seventeenth years of life, we wanted to shield her from the potential pain and grief of the world. Being aware of whatever could be happening in our daughter's teen years, at the first hint of trouble we tried to intervene. As loving parents as we tried to be, we had to face reality. Chances were that for a while our daughter would be immature as she moved through her late adolescence, unprepared for adulthood by us, her well-intentioned but controlling parents. We could have stunted her growth. It took time, worry, sleepless nights, and patience to realize that we had to withdraw our parental admonitions and observe the transitions in our daughter's life."

The reality is that there often comes a time in a loving relationship between parents and teenagers when parents have to let their children make their own decisions, not knowing everything there is to know, and stop criticizing and intervening at the first sign of trouble. It can be frustrating and even heartbreaking for parents, but the decision to limit parental knowledge and power does not come out of malice or because they don't care, but precisely the opposite—because they care enough to accept that young people need to know they are supported and have their parents' love and companionship as they explore their own world.

The above example speaks also of our relationship with God. It has long been accepted in Christian thought that God treats us like adults, that we are not God's baby dolls or play-things. Therefore, in dealing with us and supporting us to achieve our full potential, God could keep intervening, but chooses not to intervene out of love for us and out of his desire to see us grow.

After a few visits in my office and a number of heartfelt dis-cussions, Father Michael decided to take a leave of absence from his pastoral duties and go to a retreat house located in Upstate New York. He spoke seriously about his need for some solitude for personal introspection. In our last session, I gave him a list of some ideas that he could consider during his retreat. With thanks, he accepted this list and firmly shook my hand "good-bye."

FOR CONSIDERATION

1. God has created a Paradise, a perfect world for our happiness, but we messed up and made our world less than perfect. As a result of our choices, we have a world of suffering, disease, and pain; otherwise, it would be heaven. Some of these prob-lems we create ourselves, but we blame God.

2. God does not directly send pain, suffering, and disease. He does not punish us. He does not cause accidents to teach us a

lesson, although we can learn from them. God does not will earthquakes, floods, or other natural disasters. But when they happen, he gives us strength and wisdom to endure them.

3. If we take seriously that the Creator is here right now, that he is our Father—the best Father we can ever have and more, who wishes to give us everything that we need for our spiritual growth—we should feel safe, loved, accepted, harmonious, peaceful, protected, confident, and happy.

4. If you feel God isn't around, consider the possible reasons. Perhaps the two of you have not talked in a while, you might have avoided the thought of God, or you have not prayed for a long time. Could your sensitivity to his presence be affected by your preoccupation of a busy or disturbed life?

5. I think about how we actually feel when thinking about the existence of the Creator. On one hand, it is impossible to see the Creator, *for God is a Spirit,* and on the other hand, everything that exists is a manifestation of him. Over and over, God calls us to himself, to allow him to touch our life, to forgive our sins, to cleanse our life, and to give us new direction in life. If by faith we reach out to him, he will respond to the cry of our heart. He will touch us and set us free.

CHAPTER 17

Let Your Light Shine

"WE HAVE SEEN the true light, we have received the heavenly spirit" is a line from a fourth-century hymn that the early Christians sang at the end of church services. The "true light" meant Jesus Christ. When Jesus said, "I am the light of the world" (John 8:12), he meant that people would see divinity if they looked at him, not as a packet of flesh and blood, but as God. Christ is the supreme light, and it takes new eyes—the eyes of the soul—to see it.

Jesus instructed his disciples not to hide their light under a bushel basket, because they, too, were part of God. They needed to see themselves with the eyes of the soul and then let the world see how transformed they were. He says, "Let your light shine before others, so that they may see your good works and give glory to your Father in heaven" (Matt 5:16).

Our light shines when our thoughts, feelings, and actions are in agreement with the teachings of Jesus. Luke offers what is known as the Golden Rule: "Do to others as you would have them do to you" (6:31). This law tells us how Jesus wants us to live. It is also known as the Law of Love—the centerpiece of Christian faith. For people who practice this law, how do you think they might feel?

Their life would be less of a struggle.

Their wishes would be achieved more easily.

They would experience less pain and suffering.

Their soul and their spiritual life would be a real experience.

Their daily existence would be deeply meaningful.

Throughout the ages, skeptical minds have questioned God's existence. For uncertain yet sincere minds that raise this question, "Does God really exist?" the answer can take them from uncertainty—*I hope that God really exists*—to a firmer state of security—*I believe that God really exists*—and eventually to the true understanding—*I know that God really exists.*

As children, we all hoped that we would grow up to become adults. As maturity began to set in, we hoped and wished that someone would love us. In time, we believed somebody did, and now we know that we are loved.

How do we know? We found out on our own. We did not trust what others told us; we kept hoping and exploring possibilities of being loved and loving. We paid attention to our emotions and moved beyond logic into the area of intuition, insight, and wisdom. This process applies to learning how to be in relationships or even finding out our individual purpose in life.

Think of a problem that you want to solve, something deeply meaningful to you. It can be as serious as "What is my purpose in life?" or as spiritual as "Does God really love me?" You keep hoping to find an answer, but so far you haven't been able to. Whatever you choose, finding an answer that you can trust involves taking certain steps. Suppose that we apply the steps in hope to answer the question "Does God really exist?"

Step 1: Realize that our life is meant to grow and mature. In spiritual terms, growing and maturing implies accepting the presence of God as our Creator. It's a great feeling to know that our Creator is loving and sustaining us from this moment for the rest of our lives. Doubt and fear are good ingredients for spiritual growth. It is most fulfilling to know that God is real and cares for our lives. Our inner self—our soul—is delighted, knowing that God accepts and loves us unconditionally.

Step 2: Be grateful knowing we have a connection with God. By faith, our relationship or connection with God is a wonderful experience. Despite every obstacle or painful experience to which human life is subject—including corruption, crime, greed, exploitation, war, weapons, disease, and death—we can be sure that a loving God still exists. God allows humans to make mistakes and learn at their own pace. When tragedy occurs, God is present, giving courage and strength to the victims. Reality tells us that we can solve certain problems, but not all the problems that we encounter in life. Being responsible for our personal growth is far better than bemoaning the perennial state of human suffering. A Russian proverb says, "If you live near a cemetery, you cannot possibly cry for every person who dies."

Step 3: Seek what we hope, believe, and know is true. By reviewing our hopes, our beliefs, and what we really know, we will be impressed by the impact of our thoughts. In exploring our spirituality honestly, we will be surprised by the lasting joy that we experience. As a secondary benefit, we will have clarity of mind that touches our soul and senses the presence of God. Thoughts that God punishes sinners would be replaced with the reality that our sins and violations punish us—a sign of God's grace and forgiveness embracing us with love and understanding.

Step 4: Be mindful of the things we know. We inherited our belief in God from our parents or significant adults in our life. Some of us attended church and Sunday school, where we learned more about God and his creation of the world. Gradually, our beliefs became an inner conviction that there is a higher power that we call God who sustains the universe and maintains our earthly life. To know God, we need to have clarity of mind and purity of heart. Ideally, to sense God's presence, we need to have some kind of personal experience—for example, being seriously ill and experiencing healing while or after praying or being by the sea, watching the sunset and feeling a sense of awe at God's creation. The issue is not whether you have met God. The issue is your actual experience that might direct your thoughts to a world that reaches beyond the material world.

Thirty-seven years ago, I experienced severe chest pains. After thorough examination, two different cardiologists decided that I needed open-heart surgery. On the night before my surgery was scheduled, I was watching a religious program where a minister was speaking about the healing ministry of Jesus and the power of faith. I listened for a while, then turned off the TV, closed my eyes, and prayed. "Lord, I do not want to go through heart surgery. I'm afraid." After a few minutes of intense prayer, a sudden surge of bliss embraced me, and I felt relaxed and no longer afraid. The next day, when I had another test—a catheterization—a group of heart specialists decided that I did not need open-heart surgery. Besides being exuberantly happy, it was a time that I experienced God's presence as a deep inner calm and lasting joy.

Step 5: Apply what we know to our spiritual journey. The first four steps have paved the way to strengthen our hope, our belief, and our awareness. As a result, we have a basis for any possible change that we hope to see in our lives. Change requires intention and commitment.

In order to get a degree, we have to attend courses in college and read books. To get in shape, we have to be going to the gym regularly or start running, jogging, or lifting weights. We must exert ourselves until we feel a little pain, work up a sweat, and breathe hard. We may feel a little tired afterward. Similarly, in order for our spiritual life to develop and be in sound condition, simply going to church or reading the Bible—while of good benefit—is not enough. We must strive to do better, to do justice, to be honest and true, to be loving and lovable, and to muster sufficient courage to forgive people who have offended us. The main issue is to think and act in such a way that we reflect the image of God—our true spiritual selves.

We often admire beauty and love, but we rarely see them as a part of God's creation. And yet, we continually search for a greater experience of God that might transform our lives. When the space within us is not cluttered by the past and preoccupied by the future, we have a clearer vision and greater freedom to experience God.

In reality, we don't need to do too much to experience God. All we need to do is to quiet ourselves, become still. We forget all too easily that one of the big lessons of the incarnation is that God is found in the ordinary. You wish to see God? Look at the face and the eyes of the person next to you. You want to hear his voice? Listen to the cry of a baby, the loud laughter of happy people, and the wind rustling in the trees. You want to feel God? Stretch your arms out and embrace someone. God does not have human hands, but he is within you as you stretch your own hands to reach out and offer kindness, love, help, and compassion.

FOR CONSIDERATION

1. To make God real in your life, confront the serious obstacles that prevent your happiness.

2. When you feel anger or resentment against someone who has done you or someone close to you an injustice, consider the

possibility of forgiveness. In reality, forgiveness is the property of God. He is a merciful God and forgives the sinner. We often find it difficult to forgive, but when we can let go of the wrongs done to us, we truly sense the difference.

3. Do not use God as if he were a spare tire that we have just in case we need it. God is not a vague wash of emotion or a topic to postpone until a crisis looms. You will find great emotional support when you become mindful of God's constant presence in your life—a reality that your soul is ready to adapt.

4. God, the Creator of the world, is in charge of our lives. Let go and let God handle a problem or situation. Then expect the unexpected to happen. The experience that God has touched you will feel real.

5. We walk in two worlds: the material and the spiritual. In a material world, we are invited in many ways to forget God. In a spiritual world, God calls us to make an inward pilgrimage.

CHAPTER 18

The Power of Action

ALONG WITH PRAYER and faith, you may ask, "What else can I do to nurture my spiritual life?" An axiom from the ancient Greeks speaks of the human yearning: "*Syn Athena kai heiras kinei*" (Along with your prayer to goddess Athena, move your hands, take action). In other words, do something worthwhile for others. As Christians, faith must be complemented by actions: "What good is it, my brothers and sisters, if you say you have faith but do not have works? Can faith save you? If a brother or sister is naked and lacks daily food, and one of you says to them, 'Go in peace; keep warm and eat your fill,' and yet you do not supply their bodily needs, what is the good of that? So faith by itself, if it has no works, is dead" (Jas 2:14–17). James is not saying that our works make us righteous before God, but he is making it clear that real saving faith is demonstrated by good works. The same message can be found in the Gospel of Matthew: "Let your light shine before others, so that they may see your good works and give glory to your Father in heaven" (5:16).

Works may not be the cause of salvation; works are the *evidence* of salvation. The person who claims to be a Christian but lives in willful disobedience to Christ with a life that shows no works has a false or dead faith. James is clearly making a contrast between two different types of faith: true faith that saves and false faith that is dead. In other words, if people have faith, then they will produce good works. Good works are a result of faith, not a contribution to faith. A person who has genuine faith naturally does good works—God's work on earth. The good things that we do for others define our quality of faith. It is faith that works, not works that produce faith, which is why James says that a "faith by itself, if it has no works, is dead."

Faith implies action for the benefit for others, starting with our own family, our relatives, our friends, and other people. God calls us to extend his kingdom of peace and wholeness, justice, joy, and reconciliation. Through us, God is constantly at work transfiguring the world because he is a God of action. He believes in us, loves us, and wants us to have a happy and rewarding life. Our part is to share God's love with our brothers and sisters, God's children. There is no force that can resist us, no oppression that cannot be ended, no hunger that cannot be fed, no wound that cannot be healed, no hatred that cannot be turned into love, no effort to help others that cannot be fulfilled.

In the parable of the Last Judgment, Jesus says that God is not going to judge us by whether we went to church or prayed: this is not to say that these actions are unimportant, but if we go to church, if we pray, then it ought to show in how we act. When we meet hungry persons, do we offer help within our capacity? When we see people who appear thirsty, do we give them water to drink? Do we welcome the stranger and take care of the sick? As Jesus said, "Truly I tell you, just as you did it to one of the least of these who are members of my family, you did it to me" (Matt 25:40).

A church that tries to pacify its people, telling them not to concentrate on the things of this world but to think seriously of the next world, is being not only wholly irrelevant but actually against a loving God who created this world out of unfathomable love for his people. Certainly, sermons promising that there will be pie in the sky when you die do not interest me. People are starving to hear a message of God's love, his mercy, his unconditional acceptance and forgiveness, and his desire to restore those who suffer. This makes our faith real.

We can truly be grateful for what is available in our present life. Of course, as we look around and see the beauty of nature, the universe, and the masterpiece of his creation—the human being—we cannot but believe that the other world must be of equivalent beauty and indescribable magnificence. Regardless of what our fantasies or beliefs are about the next life, our finite minds cannot conceive what it will be like. However, consider the statement that Jesus made, "The kingdom of God is among you" (Luke 17:21). The kingdom of God is brought about by God and is God's gift, but it does not come without human collaboration. It needs to be proclaimed by the church in word and action so that the kingdom can break into the world more fully through the various efforts of the church on behalf of justice, peace, good works, and human reconciliation.

For a believer, a comforting definition is that the kingdom of God *is* God—insofar as God is ever present to us and to our world as a power that directs, heals, renews, re-creates, and gives life. As we recognize the kingdom of God in our midst, our responsibility is to remove the obstacles of disbelief and negative thinking. The church is not telling us to reject this vision of a final kingdom but to broaden it. God's kingdom is not simply something to be sought in the future. We are called to help bring it about now. By removing oppression, poverty, disease, and discrimination from the world, we are allowing God's kingdom and redemptive presence to be manifested now. When we pray, "Thy kingdom come," we are praying that the human family be transformed into a more just and loving community now, as well as in the world to come.

Jesus reminds his disciples that they cannot stay basking in the glory of God on the mountaintop. They must go down into the valley of human need. And so must you and I do the same. However, as we work to feed the hungry or as we try to provide help for those who are sick, we must also draw sustenance from our glimpses of God, allowing God's spirit in us to do what's needed. In all the activity that is required of us as God's partners, there must also be stillness, for in this stillness, we can hear God's voice in our lives and the will of God working in the world. The truth of the matter is that each one of us is meant to have that space in our hearts where we can hear God's voice. God is available to all of us. God says, "Be still, and know that I am God!" (Ps 46:10). We can hear God's voice most clearly when we are quiet, uncluttered, and undistracted. When we are still and at peace, we begin to hear God's voice with the ears of our heart.

When we are attentive, we might be surprised when God's voice comes to us from an unexpected source. "Expect the unexpected" has been one of my favorite axioms by Heraclitus, a Greek philosopher living 2,500 years ago. The phrase has an impact on me because it suggests being active and creative. It is the only appropriate behavior for living in such a perplexing world. If we open our hearts and minds, Heraclitus advises us, we will discover a wondrous array of ideas to help us solve the problems that inevitably fall in our path.

For example, almost five decades ago, an unexpected problem came upon me. I was a priest in the Greek Orthodox Church. Among the multiple parochial activities, an unexpected event caused great concern to our parish. Three eight-year-old boys came to America because of heart failure. Heart surgery was not practiced in Greece at that time. Of the three boys who went through open-heart surgery, two died. Performing the funerals for the two boys and trying to offer support to the grieving mothers were among the saddest moments of my ministry.

Of the many parishioners who reached out to help the grieving mothers, a Jewish woman, Rebecca Wyler, approached me and said, "Father, an article in today's newspaper told the story that an American heart surgery team had just returned from Pakistan where they performed forty-two open-heart surgeries. They are Seventh-Day Adventists. Call them. They might go to your country and do the same."

When I heard about the team's contribution and success in Pakistan, I contacted the head of the team, Dr. Ellsworth Wareham, and asked him if his team would consider going to Greece.

Hearing my story of the two boys who had died, Dr. Wareham said, "Seven of us could go to Greece and try to help as many people as possible. There will be no charge for our services, but you may have to provide traveling tickets."

After some difficulty, Olympic Airlines provided the seven tickets.

Once in Athens, the heart surgery team performed thirty-three open-heart surgeries within six weeks. Meanwhile, they examined many people and compiled a list of eight hundred young adults who needed open-heart surgery within two years.

At that time, I was the priest of Holy Trinity Greek Orthodox Church in Westfield, New Jersey. In the midst of my parochial duties, I also felt deep concern about those eight hundred people who needed immediate help. "Expect the unexpected." The words *take action* kept echoing in my brain.

I called Dr. Wareham again to ask if his heart team would consider returning to Greece. Within a week, Dr. Wareham—a man of great commitment and compassion—called back and said, "A heart surgery team of twelve will go to Greece, not just for surgery, but to train the local doctors to do open-heart surgery themselves. Now we will need twelve traveling tickets."

When I approached Olympic Airlines about the tickets, Mr. Love, the manager, said, "We gave the doctors free tickets before. We cannot give free tickets again." I left his office devastated. *What am I to tell the doctors who are ready to go to Greece and donate their services?* I kept asking myself.

Since Aristotle Onassis owned Olympic Airlines at that time, I took it upon myself to pen a letter to Mrs. Jacqueline Onassis, describing the volunteer services of the American doctors for the heart patients in Greece and requesting help.

The next day, I received a phone call at my office asking me to come to New York and to bring the names of the twelve doctors. Mrs. Onassis had ordered the manager to provide the tickets they needed.

In the five years that followed, these missionary doctors performed over one thousand open-heart surgeries at the Evangelismos Hospital in Athens and also trained the local doctors.

As their mission progressed, I asked Dr. Wareham to prepare a prospectus for a clinic of one hundred beds. He did and I brought this prospectus to the Olympic Airlines office in the hope that Mr. Onassis would see the need and build such a clinic. Aristotle Onassis left in his will that such a clinic should be built. Today, in the center of Athens, the Greek people are grateful to have the Onassis Cardiac Surgery Center.

In 2004, when I visited this magnificent seven-story cardiac surgery center, I called Dr. Wareham over the phone. With gratitude and excitement, I praised the accomplishment of his heart surgery team. His gracious reply was, "Peter, it was the work of the Holy Spirit." Who could argue the point? God works through his people to do good work for others. "Expect the unexpected."

FOR CONSIDERATION

1. Reaching out to help a person in need can give us an inner joy. It releases endorphins in our brain and boosts a lasting feeling of joy for us as well as making the person we help happy. Research shows that being kind to others increases our own levels of happiness as well as theirs. What's more, it has a knock-on effect; kindness is contagious, so it makes our communities better.

2. Recent research into brain functioning has confirmed that we are hardwired for love and compassion. So it's not all about chasing individual success. Communities and societies flourish when people look out for each other. When we're kind to people, we know that it strengthens our connections with them and provides support.

3. Doing kind things for strangers helps build cooperation, trust, and a sense of safety in our communities. It also helps us to see others more positively and empathize with them. These are the foundations of a thriving local community and a flourishing society—one that builds well-being all around.

4. Kindness can be as simple as a smile, a thank you, or a word of encouragement. It's a way of connecting, even if only for a brief moment, with those we pass in our daily lives. It doesn't have to cost anything or take much time. What's important is

that it's an act of genuine care and thoughtfulness for another person.

5. There are unlimited ways to be kind to others. We only need to keep our eyes open and pay attention to those around us to start seeing opportunities to help—a friend, a neighbor, a charitable organization, or a loved one, or because of something within us telling us to take action.

Epilogue

Now that we have come to the end of this book, you may be asking yourself: *How can I translate these thoughts into my everyday life?* There are no set answers. In fact, God's presence in our life is unique to each individual and cannot be manipulated or manufactured.

The three areas that we have reviewed—faith, prayer, and action—are intimately linked and are essential to any experience of the presence of God. It is through faith that we open ourselves to God's presence in our life. It is through prayer that we strengthen this faith and build our relationship with God so that we can be more attuned to his presence working within us. Our actions are the natural response to this presence.

The starting point is to remember that we are made in the image and likeness of God. As we grow to accept our life, we also come to accept who we really are—a human being, a child of God—and our role and purpose in creation. This acceptance requires faith, but we are also not solitary individuals, and as a result, we influence and are influenced by the lives of others with whom we come in contact. Our contribution may be small and subtle, but it is real. Being a positive force in our family, at work, and in social settings is something we all hope to achieve. Like a compass, our faith gives us our bearings and purpose. It opens the door to God, who desires that we be true to our self.

Prayer builds on faith. It is like spending time with a friend. The more time we spend with the other person, the closer we become and the more we can empathize with them and know their thoughts without the need for words. Similarly, prayer opens us to God's unconditional love and is our response to his invitation to surrender our worries and the problems that we experience. In times of crisis or when God seems distant or absent in our lives, prayer requires faith and trust in this unconditional love. Be content with whatever inspiration comes from your prayer, and remember what Jesus said: "Ask, and it will be given you; search, and you will find; knock, and the door will be opened for you" (Matt 7:7).

Finally, we are not alone on this journey. Rather, our faith and prayer is made dynamic and more vital by our interaction with others and God's creation. Our faith is strengthened not only by prayer, but also by our actions which, through faith and prayer, are our response to God's unconditional gift of blessings—grace. Furthermore, it is our actions that give flesh and meaning to our faith and make our prayer real.

Through our actions, we plant seeds of spiritual aspirations —kindness, understanding, love, generosity, and forgiveness— in the soil of human hearts. This is the kingdom of God at work within us and where we find evidence of the presence of God in our life.